Love Poems

POETRY PLEASE

Love Poems

FABER & FABER

First published in 2015
by Faber & Faber Ltd
Bloomsbury House
74–77 Great Russell Street
London WC1B 3DA

This paperback edition first published in 2016

Typeset by RefineCatch Ltd, Bungay, Suffolk
Printed and bound in England by
CPI Group (UK) Ltd, Croydon, CR0 4YY

The right of the individual authors to be identified as authors of
this work has been asserted in accordance with Section 77
of the Copyright, Designs and Patents Act 1988

A CIP record for this book
is available from the British Library

ISBN 978–0–571–32809–3

FSC
www.fsc.org
MIX
Paper from
responsible sources
FSC® C101712

2 4 6 8 10 9 7 5 3 1

Contents

᪉

POETRY PLEASE

Love Poems

Adrian Henri's Talking After Christmas Blues

Well I woke up this mornin' it was Christmas Day
And the birds were singing the night away
I saw my stocking lying on the chair
Looked right to the bottom but you weren't there
there was

>> apples
>>> oranges
>>>> chocolates
>>>>> . . . aftershave

– but no you.

So I went downstairs and the dinner was fine
There was pudding and turkey and lots of wine
And I pulled those crackers with a laughing face
Till I saw there was no one in your place
there was

>> mincepies
>>> brandy
>>>> nuts and raisins
>>>>> . . . mashed potato

– but no you.

Now it's New Year and it's Auld Lang Syne
And it's 12 o'clock and I'm feeling fine
Should Auld Acquaintance be Forgot?
I don't know girl, but it hurts a lot

there was
> whisky
> > vodka
> > > dry Martini (stirred but not shaken)
> > > > . . . and 12 New Year resolutions
– all of them about you.

So it's all the best for the year ahead
As I stagger upstairs and into bed
Then I looked at the pillow by my side
. . . I tell you baby I almost cried
there'll be
> Autumn
> Summer
> Spring
> > . . . and Winter
– all of them without you.

ADRIAN HENRI

Against Coupling

I write in praise of the solitary act:
of not feeling a trespassing tongue
forced into one's mouth, one's breath
smothered, nipples crushed against the
ribcage, and that metallic tingling
in the chin set off by a certain odd nerve:

unpleasure. Just to avoid those eyes would help –
such eyes as a young girl draws life from,
listening to the vegetal
rustle within her, as his gaze
stirs polypal fronds in the obscure
sea-bed of her body, and her own eyes blur.

There is much to be said for abandoning
this no longer novel exercise –
for not 'participating in
a total experience' – when
one feels like the lady in Leeds who
had seen *The Sound of Music* eighty-six times;

or more, perhaps, like the school drama mistress
producing *A Midsummer Night's Dream*
for the seventh year running, with
yet another cast from 5B.
Pyramus and Thisbe are dead, but
the hole in the wall can still be troublesome.

I advise you, then, to embrace it without
encumbrance. No need to set the scene,
dress up (or undress), make speeches.
Five minutes of solitude are
enough – in the bath, or to fill
that gap between the Sunday papers and lunch.

FLEUR ADCOCK

All Over Again

As if I had known you for years drink to me only if
Those frontiers have never changed on the mad map of the
   years
And all our tears were earned and this were the first cliff
From which we embraced the sea and these were the first
   words
We spread to lure the birds that nested in our day
As if it were always morning their dawnsong theirs and ours
And waking no one else me and you only now
Under the brow of a blue and imperturbable hill
Where still time stands and plays his bland and hemlock pipe
And the ripe moment tugs yet declines to fall and all
The years we had not met forget themselves in this
One kiss ingathered world and outward rippling bell
To the rim of the cup of the sky and leave it only there
Near into far blue into blue all over again
Notwithstanding unique all over all again
Of which to speak requires new fires of the tongue some trick
Of the light in the dark of the muted voice of the turning wild
World yet calm in her storm gay in her ancient rocks
To preserve today one kiss in this skybound timeless cup
Nor now shall I ask for anything more of future or past
This being last and first sound sight on eyes and ears
And each long then and there suspended on this cliff
Sinning and slicing edge that reflects the sun as if
This one Between were All and we in love for years.

LOUIS MACNEICE

The Anniversary

All kings, and all their favourites,
    All glory of honours, beauties, wits,
The sun itself, which makes times, as they pass,
Is elder by a year, now, than it was
When thou and I first one another saw:
All other things, to their destruction draw,
    Only our love hath no decay;
This, no tomorrow hath, nor yesterday,
Running it never runs from us away,
But truly keeps his first, last, everlasting day.

    Two graves must hide thine and my corse,
    If one might, death were no divorce,
Alas, as well as other princes, we
(Who prince enough in one another be,)
Must leave at last in death, these eyes, and ears,
Oft fed with true oaths, and with sweet salt tears;
    But souls where nothing dwells but love
(All other thoughts being inmates) then shall prove
This, or a love increased there above,
When bodies to their graves, souls from their graves
    remove.

    And then we shall be thoroughly blessed,
    But we no more, than all the rest.
Here upon earth, we are kings, and none but we
Can be such Kings, nor of such subjects be;
Who is so safe as we? where none can do

Treason to us, except one of us two.
    True and false fears let us refrain,
Let us love nobly, and live, and add again
Years and years unto years, till we attain
To write threescore: this is the second of our reign.

JOHN DONNE

'anyone lived in a pretty how town'

anyone lived in a pretty how town
(with up so floating many bells down)
spring summer autumn winter
he sang his didn't he danced his did.

Women and men(both little and small)
cared for anyone not at all
they sowed their isn't they reaped their same
sun moon stars rain

children guessed(but only a few
and down they forgot as up they grew
autumn winter spring summer)
that noone loved him more by more

when by now and tree by leaf
she laughed his joy she cried his grief
bird by snow and stir by still
anyone's any was all to her

someones married their everyones
laughed their cryings and did their dance
(sleep wake hope and then)they
said their nevers they slept their dream

stars rain sun moon
(and only the snow can begin to explain
how children are apt to forget to remember
with up so floating many bells down)

one day anyone died i guess
(and noone stooped to kiss his face)
busy folk buried them side by side
little by little and was by was

all by all and deep by deep
and more by more they dream their sleep
noone and anyone earth by april
wish by spirit and if by yes.

Women and men(both dong and ding)
summer autumn winter spring
reaped their sowing and went their came
sun moon stars rain

                    E. E. CUMMINGS

An Arundel Tomb

Side by side, their faces blurred,
The earl and countess lie in stone,
Their proper habits vaguely shown
As jointed armour, stiffened pleat,
And that faint hint of the absurd –
The little dogs under their feet.

Such plainness of the pre-baroque
Hardly involves the eye, until
It meets his left-hand gauntlet, still
Clasped empty in the other; and
One sees, with a sharp tender shock,
His hand withdrawn, holding her hand.

They would not think to lie so long.
Such faithfulness in effigy
Was just a detail friends would see:
A sculptor's sweet commissioned grace
Thrown off in helping to prolong
The Latin names around the base.

They would not guess how early in
Their supine stationary voyage
The air would change to soundless damage,
Turn the old tenantry away;
How soon succeeding eyes begin
To look, not read. Rigidly they

Persisted, linked, through lengths and breadths
Of time. Snow fell, undated. Light
Each summer thronged the glass. A bright
Litter of birdcalls strewed the same
Bone-riddled ground. And up the paths
The endless altered people came,

Washing at their identity.
Now, helpless in the hollow of
An unarmorial age, a trough
Of smoke in slow suspended skeins
Above their scrap of history,
Only an attitude remains:

Time has transfigured them into
Untruth. The stone fidelity
They hardly meant has come to be
Their final blazon, and to prove
Our almost-instinct almost true:
What will survive of us is love.

PHILIP LARKIN

As I Walked Out One Evening

As I walked out one evening,
     Walking down Bristol Street,
The crowds upon the pavement
     Were fields of harvest wheat.

And down by the brimming river
     I heard a lover sing
Under an arch of the railway:
     'Love has no ending.

'I'll love you, dear, I'll love you
     Till China and Africa meet,
And the river jumps over the mountain
     And the salmon sing in the street,

'I'll love you till the ocean
     Is folded and hung up to dry
And the seven stars go squawking
     Like geese about the sky.

'The years shall run like rabbits,
     For in my arms I hold
The Flower of the Ages,
     And the first love of the world.'

But all the clocks in the city
     Began to whirr and chime:
'O let not Time deceive you,
     You cannot conquer Time.

'In the burrows of the Nightmare
   Where Justice naked is,
Time watches from the shadow
   And coughs when you would kiss.

'In headaches and in worry
   Vaguely life leaks away,
And Time will have his fancy
   To-morrow or to-day.

'Into many a green valley
   Drifts the appalling snow;
Time breaks the threaded dances
   And the diver's brilliant bow.

'O plunge your hands in water,
   Plunge them in up to the wrist;
Stare, stare in the basin
   And wonder what you've missed.

'The glacier knocks in the cupboard,
   The desert sighs in the bed,
And the crack in the tea-cup opens
   A lane to the land of the dead.

'Where the beggars raffle the banknotes
   And the Giant is enchanting to Jack,
And the Lily-white Boy is a Roarer,
   And Jill goes down on her back.

'O look, look in the mirror,
   O look in your distress;

Life remains a blessing
　　Although you cannot bless.

'O stand, stand at the window
　　As the tears scald and start;
You shall love your crooked neighbour
　　With your crooked heart.'

It was late, late in the evening,
　　The lovers they were gone;
The clocks had ceased their chiming,
　　And the deep river ran on.

                              W. H. AUDEN

Atlas

There is a kind of love called maintenance,
Which stores the WD40 and knows when to use it;

Which checks the insurance, and doesn't forget
The milkman; which remembers to plant bulbs;

Which answers letters; which knows the way
The money goes; which deals with dentists

And Road Fund Tax and meeting trains,
And postcards to the lonely; which upholds

The permanently ricketty elaborate
Structures of living; which is Atlas.

And maintenance is the sensible side of love,
Which knows what time and weather are doing
To my brickwork; insulates my faulty wiring;
Laughs at my dryrotten jokes; remembers
My need for gloss and grouting; which keeps
My suspect edifice upright in air,
As Atlas did the sky.

U. A. FANTHORPE

Bar Italia

How beautiful it would be to wait for you again
in the usual place,
not looking at the door,
keeping a lookout in the long mirror,
knowing that if you are late
it will not be too late,
knowing that all I have to do
is wait a little longer
and you will be pushing through the other customers,
out of breath, apologetic.
Where have you been, for God's sake?
I was starting to worry.

How long did we say we would wait
if one of us was held up?
It's been so long and still no sign of you.
As time goes by, I search other faces in the bar,
rearranging their features
until they are monstrous versions of you,
their heads wobbling from side to side
like heads on sticks.
Your absence inches forward
until it is standing next to me.
Now it has taken the seat I was saving.
Now we are face to face in the long mirror.

HUGO WILLIAMS

A Birthday

My heart is like a singing bird
    Whose nest is in a watered shoot;
My heart is like an apple tree
    Whose boughs are bent with thickset fruit;
My heart is like a rainbow shell
    That paddles in a halcyon sea;
My heart is gladder than all these
    Because my love is come to me.

Raise me a dais of silk and down;
    Hang it with vair and purple dyes;
Carve it in doves and pomegranates,
    And peacocks with a hundred eyes;
Work it in gold and silver grapes,
    In leaves and silver fleurs-de-lys;
Because the birthday of my life
    Is come, my love is come to me.

CHRISTINA ROSSETTI

Black Monday Lovesong

In love's dances, in love's dances
One retreats and one advances.
One grows warmer and one colder,
One more hesitant, one bolder.
One gives what the other needed
Once, or will need, now unheeded.
One is clenched, compact, ingrowing
While the other's melting, flowing.
One is smiling and concealing
While the other's asking, kneeling.
One is arguing or sleeping
While the other's weeping, weeping.

And the question finds no answer
And the tune misleads the dancer
And the lost look finds no other
And the lost hand finds no brother
And the word is left unspoken
Till the theme and thread are broken.

When shall these divisions alter?
Echo's answer seems to falter:
'Oh the unperplexed, unvexed time
Next time . . . one day . . . one day . . . next time!'

A. S. J. TESSIMOND

Blindfold Games

It isn't so much that he loves her
and wants to marry her
that keeps me awake at night
as the thought of them stumbling upstairs together
in a sort of three-legged race.

I only have to close my eyes
and he is taking her by the arm,
pushing her towards the bedroom.
He has left the door half open,
but I can't quite see what they are doing,
only glimpses from time to time,
the backs of her legs, the scar on her shoulder.

I turn to look away,
but the shock of her pleasure rises in my throat,
the insult of her sweat mingling with his sweat,
her saying certain things,
her throwing out one arm.

HUGO WILLIAMS

Brand New Lover

I've abandoned vanity, since I became a body
of pixels, never quite set, since you rippled
the apparent skin of me.

I'm all texture. Silk rosette, billowing coral,
tentative as a just baked cake.
Sensations slide over my knitted blood.

My mouth is a glass paperweight
to keep our tastes in, like maraschino
cherries and water from a zinc cup.

This is not about a future
with a decorative child. Layer your pulse
onto my pulse. Dress me.

AMY KEY

Broadcast

Giant whispering and coughing from
Vast Sunday-full and organ-frowned-on spaces
Precede a sudden scuttle on the drum,
'The Queen', and huge resettling. Then begins
A snivel on the violins:
I think of your face among all those faces,

Beautiful and devout before
Cascades of monumental slithering,
One of your gloves unnoticed on the floor
Beside those new, slightly-outmoded shoes.
Here it goes quickly dark. I lose
All but the outline of the still and withering

Leaves on half-emptied trees. Behind
The glowing wavebands, rabid storms of chording
By being distant overpower my mind
All the more shamelessly, their cut-off shout
Leaving me desperate to pick out
Your hands, tiny in all that air, applauding.

PHILIP LARKIN

'Come into the Garden, Maud'

Come into the garden, Maud,
   For the black bat, night, has flown,
Come into the garden, Maud,
   I am here at the gate alone;
And the woodbine spices are wafted abroad,
   And the musk of the rose is blown.

For a breeze of morning moves,
   And the planet of Love is on high,
Beginning to faint in the light that she loves
   On a bed of daffodil sky,
To faint in the light of the sun she loves,
   To faint in his light, and to die.

All night have the roses heard
   The flute, violin, bassoon;
All night has the casement jessamine stirred
   To the dancers dancing in tune;
Till a silence fell with the waking bird,
   And a hush with the setting moon.

I said to the lily, 'There is but one
   With whom she has heart to be gay.
When will the dancers leave her alone?
   She is weary of dance and play.'
Now half to the setting moon are gone,
   And half to the rising day;
Low on the sand and loud on the stone
   The last wheel echoes away.

I said to the rose, 'The brief night goes
    In babble and revel and wine.
O young lord-lover, what sighs are those,
    For one that will never be thine?
But mine, but mine,' so I sware to the rose,
    'For ever and ever, mine.'

And the soul of the rose went into my blood,
    As the music clashed in the hall;
And long by the garden lake I stood,
    For I heard your rivulet fall
From the lake to the meadow and on to the wood,
    Our wood, that is dearer than all;

From the meadow your walks have left so sweet
    That whenever a March-wind sighs
He sets the jewel-print of your feet
    In violets blue as your eyes,
To the woody hollows in which we meet
    And the valleys of Paradise.

The slender acacia would not shake
    One long milk-bloom on the tree;
The white lake-blossom fell into the lake
    As the pimpernel dozed on the lea;
But the rose was awake all night for your sake,
    Knowing your promise to me;
The lilies and roses were all awake,
    They sighed for the dawn and thee.

Queen rose of the rosebud garden of girls,
    Come hither, the dances are done,
In gloss of satin and glimmer of pearls,
    Queen lily and rose in one;
Shine out, little head, sunning over with curls,
    To the flowers, and be their sun.

There has fallen a splendid tear
    From the passion-flower at the gate.
She is coming, my dove, my dear;
    She is coming, my life, my fate;
The red rose cries, 'She is near, she is near;'
    And the white rose weeps, 'She is late;'
The larkspur listens, 'I hear, I hear;'
    And the lily whispers, 'I wait.'

She is coming, my own, my sweet;
    Were it ever so airy a tread,
My heart would hear her and beat,
    Were it earth in an earthy bed;
My dust would hear her and beat,
    Had I lain for a century dead;
Would start and tremble under her feet,
    And blossom in purple and red.

ALFRED, LORD TENNYSON

The Confirmation

Yes, yours, my love, is the right human face.
I in my mind had waited for this long,
Seeing the false and searching for the true,
Then found you as a traveller finds a place
Of welcome suddenly amid the wrong
Valleys and rocks and twisting roads. But you,
What shall I call you? A fountain in a waste,
A well of water in a country dry,
Or anything that's honest and good, an eye
That makes the whole world bright. Your open heart,
Simple with giving, gives the primal deed,
The first good world, the blossom, the blowing seed,
The hearth, the steadfast land, the wandering sea,
Not beautiful or rare in every part,
But like yourself, as they were meant to be.

EDWIN MUIR

Counting the Beats

You, love, and I,
(He whispers) you and I,
And if no more than only you and I
What care you or I?

Counting the beats,
Counting the slow heart beats,
The bleeding to death of time in slow heart beats,
Wakeful they lie.

Cloudless day,
Night, and a cloudless day,
Yet the huge storm will burst upon their heads one day
From a bitter sky.

Where shall we be,
(She whispers) where shall we be,
When death strikes home, O where then shall we be
Who were you and I?

Not there but here,
(He whispers) only here,
As we are, here, together, now and here,
Always you and I.

Counting the beats,
Counting the slow heart beats,
The bleeding to death of time in slow heart beats,
Wakeful they lie.

ROBERT GRAVES

Delight in Disorder

A sweet disorder in the dress
Kindles in clothes a wantonness.
A lawn about the shoulders thrown
Into a fine distraction;
An erring lace, which here and there
Enthralls the crimson stomacher;
A cuff neglectful, and thereby
Ribbons to flow confusedly;
A winning wave, deserving note,
In the tempestuous petticoat;
A careless shoestring, in whose tie
I see a wild civility;
Do more bewitch me than when art
Is too precise in every part.

ROBERT HERRICK

Dining-Room Tea

When you were there, and you, and you,
Happiness crowned the night; I too,
Laughing and looking, one of all,
I watched the quivering lamplight fall
On plate and flowers and pouring tea
And cup and cloth; and they and we
Flung all the dancing moments by
With jest and glitter. Lip and eye
Flashed on the glory, shone and cried,
Improvident, unmemoried;
And fitfully and like a flame
The light of laughter went and came.
Proud in their careless transience moved
The changing faces that I loved.

Till suddenly, and otherwhence,
I looked upon your innocence.
For lifted clear and still and strange
From the dark woven flow of change
Under a vast and starless sky
I saw the immortal moment lie.
One instant I, an instant, knew
As God knows all. And it and you
I, above Time, oh, blind! could see
In witless immortality.
I saw the marble cup; the tea,
Hung on the air, an amber stream;
I saw the fire's unglittering gleam,

The painted flame, the frozen smoke.
No more the flooding lamplight broke
On flying eyes and lips and hair;
But lay, but slept unbroken there,
On stiller flesh, and body breathless,
And lips and laughter stayed and deathless,
And words on which no silence grew.
Light was more alive than you.
For suddenly, and otherwhence,
I looked on your magnificence.
I saw the stillness and the light,
And you, august, immortal, white,
Holy and strange; and every glint
Posture and jest and thought and tint
Freed from the mask of transiency,
Triumphant in eternity,
Immote, immortal.

                    Dazed at length
Human eyes grew, mortal strength
Wearied; and Time began to creep.
Change closed about me like a sleep.
Light glinted on the eyes I loved.
The cup was filled. The bodies moved.
The drifting petal came to ground.
The laughter chimed its perfect round.
The broken syllable was ended.
And I, so certain and so friended,
How could I cloud, or how distress,
The heaven of your unconsciousness?
Or shake at Time's sufficient spell,

Stammering of lights unutterable?
The eternal holiness of you,
The timeless end, you never knew,
The peace that lay, the light that shone.
You never knew that I had gone
A million miles away, and stayed
A million years. The laughter played
Unbroken round me; and the jest
Flashed on. And we that knew the best
Down wonderful hours grew happier yet.
I sang at heart, and talked, and eat,
And lived from laugh to laugh, I too,
When you were there, and you, and you.

RUPERT BROOKE

Donal Og

It is late last night the dog was speaking of you;
the snipe was speaking of you in her deep marsh.
It is you are the lonely bird through the woods;
and that you may be without a mate until you find me.

You promised me, and you said a lie to me,
that you would be before me where the sheep are flocked;
I gave a whistle and three hundred cries to you,
and I found nothing there but a bleating lamb.

You promised me a thing that was hard for you,
a ship of gold under a silver mast;
twelve towns with a market in all of them,
and a fine white court by the side of the sea.

You promised me a thing that is not possible,
that you would give me gloves of the skin of a fish;
that you would give me shoes of the skin of a bird;
and a suit of the dearest silk in Ireland.

When I go by myself to the Well of Loneliness,
I sit down and I go through my trouble;
when I see the world and do not see my boy,
he that has an amber shade in his hair.

It was on that Sunday I gave my love to you;
the Sunday that is last before Easter Sunday.
And myself on my knees reading the Passion;
and my two eyes giving love to you for ever.

My mother said to me not to be talking with you today,
or tomorrow, or on the Sunday;
it was a bad time she took for telling me that;
it was shutting the door after the house was robbed.

My heart is as black as the blackness of the sloe,
or as the black coal that is on the smith's forge;
or as the sole of a shoe left in white halls;
it was you put that darkness over my life.

You have taken the east from me; you have taken the west
    from me;
you have taken what is before me and what is behind me;
you have taken the moon, you have taken the sun from me;
and my fear is great that you have taken God from me!

ANON

From the Irish (trans. Lady Augusta Gregory)

Down by the Salley Gardens

Down by the salley gardens my love and I did meet;
She passed the salley gardens with little snow-white feet.
She bid me take love easy, as the leaves grow on the tree;
But I, being young and foolish, with her would not agree.

In a field by the river my love and I did stand,
And on my leaning shoulder she laid her snow-white hand.
She bid me take life easy, as the grass grows on the weirs;
But I was young and foolish, and now am full of tears.

W. B. YEATS

First Meeting

(to Diane)

When I first met you I knew I had come at last home,
Home after wandering, home after long puzzled searching,
Home after long being wind-borne, wave-tossed, night-
   caught,
Long being lost;

And being with you as normal and needful and natural
As sleeping or walking; and I was myself, who had never
Been wholly myself; I was walking and talking and laughing
Easily at last;

And the air was softer and sounds were sharper
And colours were brighter and the sky was higher
And length was not measured by milestones and time was
   not measured by clocks . . .
And this end was a beginning . . .
And these words are the beginning of my thanks.

A. S. J. TESSIMOND

For My Lover, Returning to his Wife

She is all there.
She was melted carefully down for you
and cast up from your childhood,
cast up from your one hundred favorite aggies.

She has always been there, my darling.
She is, in fact, exquisite.
Fireworks in the dull middle of February
and as real as a cast-iron pot.

Let's face it, I have been momentary.
A luxury. A bright red sloop in the harbor.
My hair rising like smoke from the car window.
Littleneck clams out of season.

She is more than that. She is your have to have,
has grown you your practical your tropical growth.
This is not an experiment. She is all harmony.
She sees to oars and oarlocks for the dinghy,

has placed wild flowers at the window at breakfast,
sat by the potter's wheel at midday,
set forth three children under the moon,
three cherubs drawn by Michelangelo,

done this with her legs spread out
in the terrible months in the chapel.
If you glance up, the children are there
like delicate balloons resting on the ceiling.

She has also carried each one down the hall
after supper, their heads privately bent,
two legs protesting, person to person
her face flushed with a song and their little sleep.

I give you back your heart.
I give you permission –

for the fuse inside her, throbbing
angrily in the dirt, for the bitch in her
and the burying of her wound –
for the burying of her small red wound alive –

for the pale flickering flare under her ribs,
for the drunken sailor who waits in her left pulse,
for the mother's knee, for the stockings,
for the garter belt, for the call –

the curious call
when you will burrow in arms and breasts
and tug at the orange ribbon in her hair
and answer the call, the curious call.

She is so naked and singular.
She is the sum of yourself and your dream.
Climb her like a monument, step after step.
She is solid.

As for me, I am a watercolor.
I wash off.

ANNE SEXTON

Freight

I am the ship in which you sail,
little dancing bones,
your passage between the dream
and the waking dream,
your sieve, your pea-green boat.
I'll pay whatever toll your ferry needs.
And you, whose history's already charted
in a rope of cells, be tender to
those other unnamed vessels
who will surprise you one day,
tug-tugging, irresistible,
and float you out beyond your depth,
where you'll look down, puzzled, amazed.

MAURA DOOLEY

The Geäte a-Vallèn To

In the zunsheen ov our zummers
  Wi' the haÿ time now a-come,
How busy wer we out a-vield
  Wi' vew a-left at hwome,
When waggons rumbled out ov yard
  Red wheeled, wi' body blue,
As back behind 'em loudly slamm'd
  The geäte a-vallèn to.

Drough daÿsheen ov how many years
  The geäte ha' now a-swung
Behind the veet o' vull-grown men
  An' vootsteps ov the young.
Drough years o' days it swung to us
  Behind each little shoe,
As we tripped lightly on avore
  The geäte a-vallèn to.

In evenèn time o' starry night
  How mother zot at hwome,
An' kept her bleäzèn vire bright
  Till father should ha' come,
An' how she quicken'd up an' smiled
  An' stirred her vire anew,
To hear the trampèn ho'ses' steps
  An' geäte a-vallèn to.

There's moon-sheen now in nights o' fall
　　When leaves be brown vrom green,
When, to the slammèn o' the geäte,
　　Our Jenny's ears be keen,
When the wold dog do wag his taïl,
　　An' Jeän could tell to who,
As he do come in drough the geäte,
　　The geäte a-vallèn to.

An' oft do come a saddened hour
　　When there must goo away
One well-beloved to our heart's core,
　　Vor long, perhaps vor aye:
An' oh! it is a touchèn thing
　　The lovèn heart must rue,
To hear behind his last farewell
　　The geäte a-vallèn to.

WILLIAM BARNES

[41]

The Good-Morrow

I wonder by my troth, what thou, and I
    Did, till we loved? Were we not weaned till then,
But sucked on country pleasures, childishly?
    Or snorted we in the seven sleepers' den?
'Twas so; but this, all pleasures fancies be.
If ever any beauty I did see,
Which I desired, and got, 'twas but a dream of thee.

And now good morrow to our waking souls,
    Which watch not one another out of fear;
For love, all love of other sights controls,
    And makes one little room, an every where.
Let sea-discoverers to new worlds have gone,
Let maps to others, worlds on worlds have shown:
Let us possess one world, each hath one, and is one.

My face in thine eye, thine in mine appears,
    And true plain hearts do in the faces rest:
Where can we find two better hemispheres
    Without sharp north, without declining west?
Whatever dies, was not mixed equally;
If our two loves be one, or, thou and I
Love so alike that none do slacken, none can die.

JOHN DONNE

The Great Lover

I have been so great a lover: filled my days
So proudly with the splendour of Love's praise,
The pain, the calm, and the astonishment,
Desire illimitable, and still content,
And all dear names men use, to cheat despair,
For the perplexed and viewless streams that bear
Our hearts at random down the dark of life.
Now, ere the unthinking silence on that strife
Steals down, I would cheat drowsy Death so far,
My night shall be remembered for a star
That outshone all the suns of all men's days.
Shall I not crown them with immortal praise
Whom I have loved, who have given me, dared with me
High secrets, and in darkness knelt to see
The inenarrable godhead of delight?
Love is a flame: – we have beaconed the world's night.
A city: – and we have built it, these and I.
An emperor: – we have taught the world to die.
So, for their sakes I loved, ere I go hence,
And the high cause of Love's magnificence,
And to keep loyalties young, I'll write those names
Golden for ever, eagles, crying flames,
And set them as a banner, that men may know,
To dare the generations, burn, and blow
Out on the wind of Time, shining and streaming . . .
These I have loved:

        White plates and cups, clean-gleaming,
Ringed with blue lines; and feathery, faery dust;

Wet roofs, beneath the lamp-light; the strong crust
Of friendly bread; and many-tasting food;
Rainbows; and the blue bitter smoke of wood;
And radiant raindrops couching in cool flowers;
And flowers themselves, that sway through sunny hours,
Dreaming of moths that drink them under the moon;
Then, the cool kindliness of sheets, that soon
Smooth away trouble; and the rough male kiss
Of blankets; grainy wood; live hair that is
Shining and free; blue-massing clouds; the keen
Unpassioned beauty of a great machine;
The benison of hot water; furs to touch;
The good smell of old clothes; and others such –
The comfortable smell of friendly fingers,
Hair's fragrance, and the musty reek that lingers
About dead leaves and last year's ferns . . .
                              Dear names,
And thousand other throng to me! Royal flames;
Sweet water's dimpling laugh from tap or spring;
Holes in the ground; and voices that do sing;
Voices in laughter, too; and body's pain,
Soon turned to peace; and the deep-panting train;
Firm sands; the little dulling edge of foam
That browns and dwindles as the wave goes home;
And washen stones, gay for an hour; the cold
Graveness of iron; moist black earthen mould;
Sleep; and high places; footprints in the dew;
And oaks; and brown horse-chestnuts, glossy-new;
And new-peeled sticks; and shining pools on grass; –
All these have been my loves. And these shall pass,
Whatever passes not, in the great hour,

Nor all my passion, all my prayers, have power
To hold them with me through the gate of Death.
They'll play deserter, turn with the traitor breath,
Break the high bond we made, and sell Love's trust
And sacramented covenant to the dust.
– Oh, never a doubt but, somewhere, I shall wake,
And give what's left of love again, and make
New friends, now strangers . . .
        But the best I've known
Stays here, and changes, breaks, grows old, is blown
About the winds of the world, and fades from brains
Of living men, and dies.
        Nothing remains.

O dear my loves, O faithless, once again
This one last gift I give: that after men
Shall know, and later lovers, far-removed,
Praise you, 'All these were lovely'; say, 'He loved.'

RUPERT BROOKE

Helen of Kirconnell

I wish I were where Helen lies,
Night and day on me she cries;
O that I were where Helen lies,
    On fair Kirconnell lea!

Curst be the heart that thought the thought,
And curst the hand that fired the shot,
When in my arms burd Helen dropt,
    And died to succour me!

O think na ye my heart was sair,
When my Love dropp'd and spak nae mair!
There did she swoon wi' meikle care,
    On fair Kirconnell lea.

As I went down the water side,
None but my foe to be my guide,
None but my foe to be my guide,
    On fair Kirconnell lea;

I lighted down my sword to draw,
I hackèd him in pieces sma',
I hackèd him in pieces sma',
    For her sake that died for me.

O Helen fair, beyond compare!
I'll mak a garland o' thy hair,
Shall bind my heart for evermair,
    Until the day I die!

O that I were where Helen lies!
Night and day on me she cries;
Out of my bed she bids me rise,
    Says, 'Haste, and come to me!'

O Helen fair! O Helen chaste!
If I were with thee, I'd be blest,
Where thou lies low and taks thy rest,
    On fair Kirconnell lea.

I wish my grave were growing green,
A winding-sheet drawn owre my e'en,
And I in Helen's arms lying,
    On fair Kirconnell lea.

I wish I were where Helen lies!
Night and day on me she cries;
And I am weary of the skies,
    For her sake that died for me.

ANON

Hinterhof

Stay near to me and I'll stay near to you –
As near as you are dear to me will do,
   Near as the rainbow to the rain,
   The west wind to the windowpane,
As fire to the hearth, as dawn to dew.

Stay true to me and I'll stay true to you –
As true as you are new to me will do,
   New as the rainbow in the spray,
   Utterly new in every way,
New in the way that what you say is true.

Stay near to me, stay true to me. I'll stay
As near, as true to you as heart could pray.
   Heart never hoped that one might be
   Half of the things you are to me –
The dawn, the fire, the rainbow and the day.

JAMES FENTON

'How do I love thee? Let me count the ways'

How do I love thee? Let me count the ways.
I love thee to the depth and breadth and height
My soul can reach, when feeling out of sight
For the ends of Being and ideal Grace.
I love thee to the level of everyday's
Most quiet need, by sun and candle-light.
I love thee freely, as men strive for Right;
I love thee purely, as they turn from Praise.
I love thee with the passion put to use
In my old griefs, and with my childhood's faith.
I love thee with a love I seemed to lose
With my lost saints, – I love thee with the breath,
Smiles, tears, of all my life! – and, if God choose,
I shall but love thee better after death.

ELIZABETH BARRETT BROWNING

'i carry your heart with me(i carry it in)'

i carry your heart with me(i carry it in
my heart)i am never without it(anywhere
i go you go, my dear; and whatever is done
by only me is your doing, my darling)
                                        i fear
no fate(for you are my fate,my sweet)i want
no world(for beautiful you are my world,my true)
and it's you are whatever a moon has always meant
and whatever a sun will always sing is you

here is the deepest secret nobody knows
(here is the root of the root and the bud of the bud
and the sky of the sky of a tree called life;which grows
higher than soul can hope or mind can hide)
and this is the wonder that's keeping the stars apart

i carry your heart(i carry it in my heart)

E. E. CUMMINGS

'I do not love thee!'

I do not love thee! – no! I do not love thee!
And yet when thou art absent I am sad;
    And envy even the bright blue sky above thee,
Whose quiet stars may see thee and be glad.

I do not love thee! – yet, I know not why,
Whate'er thou dost seems still well done, to me –
    And often in my solitude I sigh –
That those I do love are not more like thee!

I do not love thee! – yet, when thou art gone
I hate the sound (though those who speak be dear)
    Which breaks the lingering echo of the tone
Thy voice of music leaves upon my ear.

I do not love thee! – yet thy speaking eyes,
With their deep, bright, and most expressive blue –
    Between me and the midnight heaven arise,
Oftener than any eyes I ever knew.

I know I do not love thee! – yet, alas!
Others will scarcely trust my candid heart;
    And oft I catch them smiling as they pass,
Because they see me gazing where thou art.

CAROLINE NORTON

I Leave This at Your Ear

For Nessie Dunsmuir

I leave this at your ear for when you wake,
A creature in its abstract cage asleep.
Your dreams blindfold you by the light they make.

The owl called from the naked-woman tree
As I came down by the Kyle farm to hear
Your house silent by the speaking sea.

I have come late but I have come before
Later with slaked steps from stone to stone
To hope to find you listening for the door.

I stand in the ticking room. My dear, I take
A moth kiss from your breath. The shore gulls cry.
I leave this at your ear for when you wake.

W. S. GRAHAM

If I Could Tell You

Time will say nothing but I told you so,
Time only knows the price we have to pay;
If I could tell you I would let you know.

If we should weep when clowns put on their show,
If we should stumble when musicians play,
Time will say nothing but I told you so.

There are no fortunes to be told, although,
Because I love you more than I can say,
If I could tell you I would let you know.

The winds must come from somewhere when
   they blow,
There must be reasons why the leaves decay;
Time will say nothing but I told you so.

Perhaps the roses really want to grow,
The vision seriously intends to stay;
If I could tell you I would let you know.

Suppose the lions all get up and go,
And all the brooks and soldiers run away;
Will Time say nothing but I told you so?
If I could tell you I would let you know.

W. H. AUDEN

In a Bath Teashop

'Let us not speak, for the love we bear one another –
 Let us hold hands and look.'
She, such a very ordinary little woman;
 He, such a thumping crook;
But both, for a moment, little lower than the angels
 In the teashop's ingle-nook.

JOHN BETJEMAN

In Paris with You

Don't talk to me of love. I've had an earful
And I get tearful when I've downed a drink or two.
I'm one of your talking wounded.
I'm a hostage. I'm maroonded.
But I'm in Paris with you.

Yes I'm angry at the way I've been bamboozled
And resentful at the mess that I've been through.
I admit I'm on the rebound
And I don't care where are we bound.
I'm in Paris with you.

Do you mind if we do not go to the Louvre,
If we say sod off to sodding Notre Dame,
If we skip the Champs Elysées
And remain here in this sleazy
Old hotel room
Doing this and that
To what and whom
Learning who you are,
Learning what I am.

Don't talk to me of love. Let's talk of Paris,
The little bit of Paris in our view.
There's that crack across the ceiling
And the hotel walls are peeling
And I'm in Paris with you.

Don't talk to me of love. Let's talk of Paris.
I'm in Paris with the slightest thing you do.
I'm in Paris with your eyes, your mouth,
I'm in Paris with . . . all points south.
Am I embarrassing you?
I'm in Paris with you.

JAMES FENTON

In the Orchard

'I thought you loved me.' 'No, it was only fun.'
'When we stood there, closer than all?' 'Well, the harvest moon
Was shining and queer in your hair, and it turned my head.'
'That made you?' 'Yes.' 'Just the moon and the light it made
Under the tree?' 'Well, your mouth, too.' 'Yes, my mouth?'
'And the quiet there that sang like the drum in the booth.
You shouldn't have danced like that.' 'Like what?' 'So close,
With your head turned up, and the flower in your hair, a rose
That smelt all warm.' 'I loved you. I thought you knew
I wouldn't have danced like that with any but you.'
'I didn't know. I thought you knew it was fun.'
'I thought it was love you meant.' 'Well, it's done.' 'Yes, it's
    done.
I've seen boys stone a blackbird, and watched them drown
A kitten . . . it clawed at the reeds, and they pushed it down
Into the pool while it screamed. Is that fun, too?'
'Well, boys are like that . . . Your brothers . . .' 'Yes, I know.
But you, so lovely and strong! Not you! Not you!'
'They don't understand it's cruel. It's only a game.'
'And are girls fun, too?' 'No, still in a way it's the same.
It's queer and lovely to have a girl . . .' 'Go on.'
'It makes you mad for a bit to feel she's your own,
And you laugh and kiss her, and maybe you give her a ring,
But it's only in fun.' 'But I gave you everything.'
'Well, you shouldn't have done it. You know what a fellow
    thinks
When a girl does that.' 'Yes, he talks of her over his drinks
And calls her a – ' 'Stop that now. I thought you knew.'

'But it wasn't with anyone else. It was only you.'
'How did I know? I thought you wanted it too.
I thought you were like the rest. Well, what's to be done?'
'To be done?' 'Is it all right?' 'Yes.' 'Sure?' 'Yes, but why?'
'I don't know. I thought you were going to cry.
You said you had something to tell me.' 'Yes, I know.
It wasn't anything really . . . I think I'll go.'
'Yes, it's late. There's thunder about, a drop of rain
Fell on my hand in the dark. I'll see you again
At the dance next week. You're sure that everything's right?'
'Yes.' 'Well, I'll be going.' 'Kiss me . . .' 'Good night.' . . .
    'Good night.'

MURIEL STUART

Jenny Kissed Me

Jenny kissed me when we met,
   Jumping from the chair she sat in;
Time, you thief, who love to get
   Sweets into your list, put that in!
Say I'm weary, say I'm sad,
   Say that health and wealth have missed me,
Say I'm growing old, but add,
   Jenny kissed me.

LEIGH HUNT

La Belle Dame Sans Merci

Ah, what can ail thee, wretched wight,
   Alone and palely loitering;
The sedge is wither'd from the lake,
   And no birds sing.

Ah, what can ail thee, wretched wight,
   So haggard and so woe-begone?
The squirrel's granary is full,
   And the harvest's done.

I see a lilly on thy brow,
   With anguish moist and fever dew;
And on thy cheek a fading rose
   Fast withereth too.

I met a lady in the meads
   Full beautiful, a faery's child;
Her hair was long, her foot was light,
   And her eyes were wild.

I set her on my pacing steed,
    And nothing else saw all day long;
For sideways would she lean, and sing
    A faery's song.

VI

I made a garland for her head,
    And bracelets too, and fragrant zone;
She look'd at me as she did love,
    And made sweet moan.

VII

She found me roots of relish sweet,
    And honey wild, and manna dew;
And sure in language strange she said,
    I love thee true.

VIII

She took me to her elfin grot,
    And there she gaz'd and sighed deep,
And there I shut her wild sad eyes –
    So kiss'd to sleep.

IX

And there we slumber'd on the moss,
    And there I dream'd, ah woe betide,
The latest dream I ever dream'd
    On the cold hill side.

I saw pale kings, and princes too,
   Pale warriors, death-pale were they all;
Who cry'd – 'La belle Dame sans merci
   Hath thee in thrall!'

XI

I saw their starv'd lips in the gloam
   With horrid warning gaped wide,
And I awoke, and found me here
   On the cold hill side.

XII

And this is why I sojourn here
   Alone and palely loitering,
Though the sedge is wither'd from the lake,
   And no birds sing.

JOHN KEATS

La Figlia Che Piange

O quam te memorem virgo . . .

Stand on the highest pavement of the stair –
Lean on a garden urn –
Weave, weave the sunlight in your hair –
Clasp your flowers to you with a pained surprise –
Fling them to the ground and turn
With a fugitive resentment in your eyes:
But weave, weave the sunlight in your hair.

So I would have had him leave,
So I would have had her stand and grieve,
So he would have left
As the soul leaves the body torn and bruised,
As the mind deserts the body it has used.
I should find
Some way incomparably light and deft,
Some way we both should understand,
Simple and faithless as a smile and shake of the hand.

She turned away, but with the autumn weather
Compelled my imagination many days,
Many days and many hours:
Her hair over her arms and her arms full of flowers.
And I wonder how they should have been together!
I should have lost a gesture and a pose.
Sometimes these cogitations still amaze
The troubled midnight and the noon's repose.

T. S. ELIOT

[63]

The Lady of Shalott

I

On either side the river lie
Long fields of barley and of rye,
That clothe the wold and meet the sky;
And thro' the field the road runs by
     To many-tower'd Camelot;
And up and down the people go,
Gazing where the lilies blow
Round an island there below,
     The island of Shalott.

Willows whiten, aspens quiver,
Little breezes dusk and shiver
Thro' the wave that runs for ever
By the island in the river
     Flowing down to Camelot.
Four gray walls, and four gray towers,
Overlook a space of flowers,
And the silent isle imbowers
     The Lady of Shalott.

By the margin, willow-veil'd,
Slide the heavy barges trail'd
By slow horses; and unhail'd
The shallop flitteth silken-sail'd
     Skimming down to Camelot:
But who hath seen her wave her hand?

Or at the casement seen her stand?
Or is she known in all the land,
    The Lady of Shalott?

Only reapers, reaping early
In among the bearded barley,
Hear a song that echoes cheerly
From the river winding clearly,
    Down to tower'd Camelot:
And by the moon the reaper weary,
Piling sheaves in uplands airy,
Listening, whispers ''Tis the fairy
    Lady of Shalott.'

II

There she weaves by night and day
A magic web with colours gay.
She has heard a whisper say,
A curse is on her if she stay
    To look down to Camelot.
She knows not what the curse may be,
And so she weaveth steadily,
And little other care hath she,
    The Lady of Shalott.

And moving thro' a mirror clear
That hangs before her all the year,
Shadows of the world appear.
There she sees the highway near
    Winding down to Camelot:
There the river eddy whirls,

And there the surly village-churls,
And the red cloaks of market girls,
  Pass onward from Shalott.

Sometimes a troop of damsels glad,
An abbot on an ambling pad,
Sometimes a curly shepherd-lad,
Or long-hair'd page in crimson clad,
  Goes by to tower'd Camelot;
And sometimes thro' the mirror blue
The knights come riding two and two:
She hath no loyal knight and true,
  The Lady of Shalott.

But in her web she still delights
To weave the mirror's magic sights,
For often thro' the silent nights
A funeral, with plumes and lights
  And music, went to Camelot:
Or when the moon was overhead,
Came two young lovers lately wed;
'I am half sick of shadows,' said
  The Lady of Shalott.

III

A bow-shot from her bower-eaves.
He rode between the barley-sheaves,
The sun came dazzling thro' the leaves,
And flamed upon the brazen greaves
  Of bold Sir Lancelot.

A red-cross knight for ever kneel'd
To a lady in his shield,
That sparkled on the yellow field,
    Beside remote Shalott.

The gemmy bridle glitter'd free,
Like to some branch of stars we see
Hung in the golden Galaxy.
The bridle bells rang merrily
    As he rode down to Camelot:
And from his blazon'd baldric slung
A mighty silver bugle hung,
And as he rode his armour rung,
    Beside remote Shalott.

All in the blue unclouded weather
Thick-jewell'd shone the saddle-leather,
The helmet and the helmet-feather
Burn'd like one burning flame together,
    As he rode down to Camelot.
As often thro' the purple night,
Below the starry clusters bright,
Some bearded meteor, trailing light,
    Moves over still Shalott.

His broad clear brow in sunlight glow'd;
On burnish'd hooves his war-horse trode;
From underneath his helmet flow'd
His coal-black curls as on he rode,
    As he rode down to Camelot.
From the bank and from the river

He flash'd into the crystal mirror,
'Tirra lirra,' by the river
  Sang Sir Lancelot.

She left the web, she left the loom,
She made three paces thro' the room,
She saw the water-lily bloom,
She saw the helmet and the plume,
  She look'd down to Camelot.
Out flew the web and floated wide;
The mirror crack'd from side to side;
'The curse is come upon me,' cried
  The Lady of Shalott.

IV

In the stormy east-wind straining,
The pale yellow woods were waning,
The broad stream in his banks complaining,
Heavily the low sky raining
  Over tower'd Camelot;
Down she came and found a boat
Beneath a willow left afloat,
And round about the prow she wrote
  The Lady of Shalott.

And down the river's dim expanse
Like some bold seër in a trance,
Seeing all his own mischance –
With a glassy countenance
  Did she look to Camelot.
And at the closing of the day

She loosed the chain, and down she lay;
The broad stream bore her far away,
    The Lady of Shalott.

Lying, robed in snowy white
That loosely flew to left and right –
The leaves upon her falling light –
Thro' the noises of the night
    She floated down to Camelot:
And as the boat-head wound along
The willowy hills and fields among,
They heard her singing her last song,
    The Lady of Shalott.

Heard a carol, mournful, holy,
Chanted loudly, chanted lowly,
Till her blood was frozen slowly,
And her eyes were darken'd wholly,
    Turn'd to tower'd Camelot.
For ere she reach'd upon the tide
The first house by the water-side,
Singing in her song she died,
    The Lady of Shalott.

Under tower and balcony,
By garden-wall and gallery,
A gleaming shape she floated by,
Dead-pale between the houses high,
    Silent into Camelot.
Out upon the wharfs they came,
Knight and burgher, lord and dame,

And round the prow they read her name,
The Lady of Shalott.

Who is this? and what is here?
And in the lighted palace near
Died the sound of royal cheer;
And they cross'd themselves for fear,
　　All the knights at Camelot:
But Lancelot mused a little space;
He said, 'She has a lovely face;
God in his mercy lend her grace,
　　The Lady of Shalott.'

ALFRED, LORD TENNYSON

Late Fragment

And did you get what
you wanted from this life, even so?
I did.
And what did you want?
To call myself beloved, to feel myself
beloved on the earth.

RAYMOND CARVER

'Let me not to the marriage of true minds'

Let me not to the marriage of true minds
Admit impediments; love is not love
Which alters when it alteration finds,
Or bends with the remover to remove.
O no, it is an ever-fixèd mark
That looks on tempests and is never shaken;
It is the star to every wandering bark,
Whose worth's unknown, although his height be taken.
Love's not Time's fool, though rosy lips and cheeks
Within his bending sickle's compass come;
Love alters not with his brief hours and weeks,
But bears it out even to the edge of doom.
   If this be error and upon me proved,
   I never writ, nor no man ever loved.

WILLIAM SHAKESPEARE

'Let me put it this way'

Let me put it this way:
if you came to lay

your sleeping head
against my arm or sleeve,

and if my arm went dead,
or if I had to take my leave

at midnight, I should rather
cleave it from the joint or seam

than make a scene
or bring you round.

There,
how does that sound?

SIMON ARMITAGE

Letter to Husband

Dearest husband   Beloved husband   Most respected
missed and righteous husband   Dear treasured, absent
husband   Dear unimaginable piece of husband
Dear husband of the moon,   it has been six months since I
Dear much lamented distant husband, my champing   heart
forgives you   please come.   In a long
undergrowth of wanting I creep   at night the sea is a dark room
I called and called   These white corridors are not
free from longing   Dear postman   Dear night-time, dear
dark mouth hovering over me   Dear knee bones
dear palms, dear faithful   body   I have wants

Husband –   Speech is a dark stain spreading
I have no telephone   No one will give me a telephone
I lost your voice   in dark places   it is written
over and over   that   please come.
A scribble is the way a heartbeat is told   Dearest serrated
husband. My heartscribbles   your name. My mouth
scribbles: I have cried your name in every
possible colour I have given you my proud   desperate
undeviating wish   over and over and over: Sweetheart, please come

EMILY BERRY

The Linen Industry

Pulling up flax after the blue flowers have fallen
And laying our handfuls in the peaty water
To rot those grasses to the bone, or building stooks
That recall the skirts of an invisible dancer,

We become a part of the linen industry
And follow its processes to the grubby town
Where fields are compacted into window-boxes
And there is little room among the big machines.

But even in our attic under the skylight
We make love on a bleach green, the whole meadow
Draped with material turning white in the sun
As though snow reluctant to melt were our attire.

What's passion but a battering of stubborn stalks,
Then a gentle combing out of fibres like hair
And a weaving of these into christening robes,
Into garments for a marriage or funeral?

Since it's like a bereavement once the labour's done
To find ourselves last workers in a dying trade,
Let flax be our matchmaker, our undertaker,
The provider of sheets for whatever the bed –

And be shy of your breasts in the presence of death,
Say that you look more beautiful in linen
Wearing white petticoats, the bow on your bodice
A butterfly attending the embroidered flowers.

MICHAEL LONGLEY

Litany

You are the bread and the knife,
The crystal goblet and the wine . . .

JACQUES CRICKILLON

You are the bread and the knife,
the crystal goblet and the wine.
You are the dew on the morning grass
and the burning wheel of the sun.
You are the white apron of the baker,
and the marsh birds suddenly in flight.

However, you are not the wind in the orchard,
the plums on the counter,
or the house of cards.
And you are certainly not the pine-scented air.
There is just no way that you are the pine-scented air.

It is possible that you are the fish under the bridge,
maybe even the pigeon on the general's head,
but you are not even close
to being the field of cornflowers at dusk.

And a quick look in the mirror will show
that you are neither the boots in the corner
nor the boat asleep in its boathouse.

It might interest you to know,
speaking of the plentiful imagery of the world,
that I am the sound of rain on the roof.

I also happen to be the shooting star,
the evening paper blowing down an alley
and the basket of chestnuts on the kitchen-table.

I am also the moon in the trees
and the blind woman's tea cup.
But don't worry, I'm not the bread and the knife.
You are still the bread and the knife.
You will always be the bread and the knife,
not to mention the crystal goblet and – somehow – the wine.

BILLY COLLINS

Litany

for Robin Robertson

Dear god,
        let me remember these months of transition
in a room on the Harrow Road, the traffic
muffled by a plastic sheet, the facing ziggurats
with their satellite dishes and tea-towels out to dry,
a lengthwise Brazilian flag curtaining one window,

indigents and fellow aliens and oddballs in the street,
the wobbly eyes I mistakenly looked into, wobbly and then
suddenly murderous, the fat friendly ladies and truanting
    children,
West Indian barbers and Lebanese grocers eating on the job,
the line of a hundred people outside the post office
at a minute to nine on Monday morning,

the pallet, table and two chairs
in the room at the top of the sharp and loose coir staircase,
a kettle and ashtray before I remembered about food,
the streetlamp almost within reach to slide down, fireman-
    style,
im Falle eines Falles,
the reflections of car windscreens bouncing on the ceiling,

the solicitous Irish landlady, Marie's sister, saying
'Are you alright? Now are you sure you're alright?'
the canal at the back, seedy as Xochimilco,

the May air full of seeds, alder and plane and sycamore,
generative fluff, myself fluffy and generative,
wild-haired and with the taste of L. in my mouth,
the office workers opposite
very evidently pissing behind milk-glass,
goslings and baby coots without the white stripe as yet,
attack dogs defecating on the grass,
the occasional putter of narrow boats, industrial
and bucolic as canals are industrial and bucolic,

the velvet curtains slowly turning to dust on the
    woodwormed rail,
my diminished establishment of bin-liners and suitcase
(our 1961 cardboard family 'Revelation'),
the Olympia Traveller I lugged around Mexico and two pairs
    of boots,
otherwise silence and light and dust and flies,
so hungry I picked the bin when I visited my children,

the steel doors and squats of Walterton and Elgin
from the days before pastel paint, a hulking unmistakable
    school
on the light industrial skyline, barbed wire, coupling pigeons,
yellow brick and corrugated Homebase prefab, living for
    nightfall
and the bus that took me round the houses
to heaven.

MICHAEL HOFMANN

Love

Thou art too hard for me in Love:
There is no dealing with thee in that Art:
    That is thy Masterpiece I see.
    When I contrive and plot to prove
Something that may be conquest on my part
    Thou still, O Lord, outstrippest me.

Sometimes, when as I wash, I say
And shrewdly, as I think, Lord wash my soul
    More spotted than my flesh can be.
    But then there comes into my way
Thy ancient baptism, which when I was foul
    And knew it not, yet cleansed me.

I took a time when thou didst sleep,
Great waves of trouble combating my breast:
    I thought it brave to praise thee then,
    Yet then I found, that thou didst creep
Into my heart with joy, giving more rest
    Than flesh did lend thee, back again.

Let me but once the conquest have
Upon the matter, 'twill thy conquest prove:
    If thou subdue mortality
    Thou dost no more, than doth the grave:
Whereas if I o'ercome thee and thy Love
    Hell, Death and Devil come short of me.

GEORGE HERBERT

Love Among the Ruins

Where the quiet-coloured end of evening smiles,
  Miles and miles
On the solitary pastures where our sheep
  Half-asleep
Tinkle homeward thro' the twilight, stray or stop
  As they crop –
Was the site once of a city great and gay,
  (So they say)
Of our country's very capital, its prince
  Ages since
Held his court in, gathered councils, wielding far
  Peace or war.

Now, – the country does not even boast a tree
  As you see,
To distinguish slopes of verdure, certain rills
  From the hills
Intersect and give a name to, (else they run
  Into one)
Where the domed and daring palace shot its spires
  Up like fires
O'er the hundred-gated circuit of a wall
  Bounding all,
Made of marble, men might march on nor be pressed
  Twelve abreast.

And such plenty and perfection, see, of grass
  Never was!
Such a carpet as, this summer-time, o'erspreads

And embeds
Every vestige of the city, guessed alone,
   Stock or stone –
Where a multitude of men breathed joy and woe
   Long ago;
Lust of glory pricked their hearts up, dread of shame
   Struck them tame;
And that glory and that shame alike, the gold
   Bought and sold.

Now, – the single little turret that remains
   On the plains,
By the caper overrooted, by the gourd
   Overscored,
While the patching houseleek's head of blossom winks
   Through the chinks –
Marks the basement whence a tower in ancient time
   Sprang sublime,
And a burning ring, all round, the chariots traced
   As they raced,
And the monarch and his minions and his dames
   Viewed the games.

And I know, while thus the quiet-coloured eve
   Smiles to leave
To their folding, all our many-tinkling fleece
   In such peace,
And the slopes and rills in undistinguished grey
   Melt away –
That a girl with eager eyes and yellow hair
   Waits me there
In the turret whence the charioteers caught soul

For the goal,
When the king looked, where she looks now, breathless,
    dumb
    Till I come.

But he looked upon the city, every side,
    Far and wide,
All the mountains topped with temples, all the glades'
    Colonnades,
All the causeys, bridges, aqueducts, – and then,
    All the men!
When I do come, she will speak not, she will stand,
    Either hand
On my shoulder, give her eyes the first embrace
    Of my face,
Ere we rush, ere we extinguish sight and speech
    Each on each.

In one year they sent a million fighters forth
    South and North,
And they built their gods a brazen pillar high
    As the sky,
Yet reserved a thousand chariots in full force –
    Gold, of course.
Oh heart! oh blood that freezes, blood that burns!
    Earth's returns
For whole centuries of folly, noise and sin!
    Shut them in,
With their triumphs and their glories and the rest!
    Love is best.

ROBERT BROWNING

The Love Song of J. Alfred Prufrock

S'io credessi che mia risposta fosse
a persona che mai tornasse al mondo,
questa fiamma staria senza più scosse.
Ma per ciò che giammai di questo fondo
non tornò vivo alcun, s'i'odo il vero,
senza tema d'infamia ti rispondo.

Let us go then, you and I,
When the evening is spread out against the sky
Like a patient etherised upon a table;
Let us go, through certain half-deserted streets,
The muttering retreats
Of restless nights in one-night cheap hotels
And sawdust restaurants with oyster-shells:
Streets that follow like a tedious argument
Of insidious intent
To lead you to an overwhelming question . . .
Oh, do not ask, 'What is it?'
Let us go and make our visit.

In the room the women come and go
Talking of Michelangelo.

The yellow fog that rubs its back upon the window-panes,
The yellow smoke that rubs its muzzle on the window-panes,
Licked its tongue into the corners of the evening,
Lingered upon the pools that stand in drains,
Let fall upon its back the soot that falls from chimneys,
    Slipped by the terrace, made a sudden leap,
And seeing that it was a soft October night,
Curled once about the house, and fell asleep.

And indeed there will be time
For the yellow smoke that slides along the street
Rubbing its back upon the window-panes;
There will be time, there will be time
To prepare a face to meet the faces that you meet;
There will be time to murder and create,
And time for all the works and days of hands
That lift and drop a question on your plate;
Time for you and time for me,
And time yet for a hundred indecisions,
And for a hundred visions and revisions,
Before the taking of a toast and tea.

In the room the women come and go
Talking of Michelangelo.

And indeed there will be time
To wonder, 'Do I dare?' and, 'Do I dare?'
Time to turn back and descend the stair,
With a bald spot in the middle of my hair –
(They will say: 'How his hair is growing thin!')
My morning coat, my collar mounting firmly to the chin,
My necktie rich and modest, but asserted by a simple pin –
(They will say: 'But how his arms and legs are thin!')
Do I dare
Disturb the universe?
In a minute there is time
For decisions and revisions which a minute will reverse.
For I have known them all already, known them all –
Have known the evenings, mornings, afternoons,
I have measured out my life with coffee spoons;

I know the voices dying with a dying fall
Beneath the music from a farther room.
    So how should I presume?

And I have known the eyes already, known them all –
The eyes that fix you in a formulated phrase,
And when I am formulated, sprawling on a pin,
When I am pinned and wriggling on the wall,
Then how should I begin
To spit out all the butt-ends of my days and ways?
    And how should I presume?

And I have known the arms already, known them all –
Arms that are braceleted and white and bare
(But in the lamplight, downed with light brown hair!)
Is it perfume from a dress
That makes me so digress?
Arms that lie along a table, or wrap about a shawl.
    And should I then presume?
    And how should I begin?

                .   .   .   .   .

Shall I say, I have gone at dusk through narrow streets
And watched the smoke that rises from the pipes
Of lonely men in shirt-sleeves, leaning out of windows? . . .

I should have been a pair of ragged claws
Scuttling across the floors of silent seas.

                .   .   .   .   .

And the afternoon, the evening, sleeps so peacefully!
Smoothed by long fingers,
Asleep . . . tired . . . or it malingers,
Stretched on the floor, here beside you and me.
Should I, after tea and cakes and ices,
Have the strength to force the moment to its crisis?
But though I have wept and fasted, wept and prayed,
Though I have seen my head (grown slightly bald)
    brought in upon a platter,
I am no prophet – and here's no great matter;
I have seen the moment of my greatness flicker,
And I have seen the eternal Footman hold my coat,
    and snicker,
And in short, I was afraid.

And would it have been worth it, after all,
After the cups, the marmalade, the tea,
Among the porcelain, among some talk of you and me,
Would it have been worth while,
To have bitten off the matter with a smile,
To have squeezed the universe into a ball
To roll it towards some overwhelming question,
To say: 'I am Lazarus, come from the dead,
Come back to tell you all, I shall tell you all' –
If one, settling a pillow by her head,
    Should say: 'That is not what I meant at all.
    That is not it, at all.'

And would it have been worth it, after all,
Would it have been worth while,
After the sunsets and the dooryards and the sprinkled
    streets,

After the novels, after the teacups, after the skirts that trail
    along the floor –
And this, and so much more? –
It is impossible to say just what I mean!
But as if a magic lantern threw the nerves in patterns on
    a screen:
Would it have been worth while
If one, settling a pillow or throwing off a shawl,
And turning toward the window, should say:
    'That is not it at all,
    That is not what I meant at all.'

.   .   .   .   .

No! I am not Prince Hamlet, nor was meant to be;
Am an attendant lord, one that will do
To swell a progress, start a scene or two,
Advise the prince; no doubt, an easy tool,
Deferential, glad to be of use,
Politic, cautious, and meticulous;
Full of high sentence, but a bit obtuse;
At times, indeed, almost ridiculous –
Almost, at times, the Fool.

I grow old . . . I grow old . . .
I shall wear the bottoms of my trousers rolled.

Shall I part my hair behind? Do I dare to eat a peach?
I shall wear white flannel trousers, and walk upon the beach.
I have heard the mermaids singing, each to each.

I do not think that they will sing to me.

I have seen them riding seaward on the waves
Combing the white hair of the waves blown back
When the wind blows the water white and black.

We have lingered in the chambers of the sea
By sea-girls wreathed with seaweed red and brown
Till human voices wake us, and we drown.

T. S. ELIOT

Love Songs in Age

She kept her songs, they took so little space,
The covers pleased her:
One bleached from lying in a sunny place,
One marked in circles by a vase of water,
One mended, when a tidy fit had seized her,
And coloured, by her daughter –
So they had waited, till in widowhood
She found them, looking for something else, and stood

Relearning how each frank submissive chord
Had ushered in
Word after sprawling hyphenated word,
And the unfailing sense of being young
Spread out like a spring-woken tree, wherein
That hidden freshness sung,
That certainty of time laid up in store
As when she played them first. But, even more,

The glare of that much-mentioned brilliance, love,
Broke out, to show
Its bright incipience sailing above,
Still promising to solve, and satisfy,
And set unchangeably in order. So
To pile them back, to cry,
Was hard, without lamely admitting how
It had not done so then, and could not now.

PHILIP LARKIN

Love Without Hope

Love without hope, as when the young bird-catcher
Swept off his tall hat to the Squire's own daughter,
So let the imprisoned larks escape and fly
Singing about her head, as she rode by.

ROBERT GRAVES

The Lover Writes a One-Word Poem

You!

GAVIN EWART

Lovesong

He loved her and she loved him
His kisses sucked out her whole past and future or tried to
He had no other appetite
She bit him she gnawed him she sucked
She wanted him complete inside her
Safe and sure forever and ever
Their little cries fluttered into the curtains

Her eyes wanted nothing to get away
Her looks nailed down his hands his wrists his elbows
He gripped her hard so that life
Should not drag her from that moment
He wanted all future to cease
He wanted to topple with his arms round her
Off that moment's brink and into nothing
Or everlasting or whatever there was
Her embrace was an immense press
To print him into her bones
His smiles were the garrets of a fairy palace
Where the real world would never come
Her smiles were spider bites
So he would lie still till she felt hungry
His words were occupying armies
Her laughs were an assassin's attempts
His looks were bullets daggers of revenge
Her glances were ghosts in the corner with horrible secrets
His whispers were whips and jackboots
Her kisses were lawyers steadily writing

His caresses were the last hooks of a castaway
Her love-tricks were the grinding of locks
And their deep cries crawled over the floors
Like an animal dragging a great trap

His promises were the surgeon's gag
Her promises took the top off his skull
She would get a brooch made of it
His vows pulled out all her sinews
He showed her how to make a love-knot
Her vows put his eyes in formalin
At the back of her secret drawer
Their screams stuck in the wall
Their heads fell apart into sleep like the two halves
Of a lopped melon, but love is hard to stop

In their entwined sleep they exchanged arms and legs
In their dreams their brains took each other hostage

In the morning they wore each other's face

TED HUGHES

Lullaby

Lay your sleeping head, my love,
Human on my faithless arm;
Time and fevers burn away
Individual beauty from
Thoughtful children, and the grave
Proves the child ephemeral:
But in my arms till break of day
Let the living creature lie,
Mortal, guilty, but to me
The entirely beautiful.

Soul and body have no bounds:
To lovers as they lie upon
Her tolerant enchanted slope
In their ordinary swoon,
Grave the vision Venus sends
Of supernatural sympathy,
Universal love and hope;
While an abstract insight wakes
Among the glaciers and the rocks
The hermit's sensual ecstasy.

Certainty, fidelity
On the stroke of midnight pass
Like vibrations of a bell,
And fashionable madmen raise
Their pedantic boring cry:
Every farthing of the cost,

All the dreaded cards foretell,
Shall be paid, but from this night
Not a whisper, not a thought,
Not a kiss nor look be lost.

Beauty, midnight, vision dies:
Let the winds of dawn that blow
Softly round your dreaming head
Such a day of sweetness show
Eye and knocking heart may bless,
Find the mortal world enough;
Noons of dryness see you fed
By the involuntary powers,
Nights of insult let you pass
Watched by every human love.

W. H. AUDEN

Machines

Dearest, note how these two are alike:
This harpsichord pavane by Purcell
And the racer's twelve-speed bike.

The machinery of grace is always simple.
This chrome trapezoid, one wheel connected
To another of concentric gears,
Which Ptolemy dreamt of and Schwinn perfected,
Is gone. The cyclist, not the cycle, steers.
And in the playing, Purcell's chords are played away.

So this talk, or touch if I were there,
Should work its effortless gadgetry of love,
Like Dante's heaven, and melt into the air.

If it doesn't, of course, I've fallen. So much is chance,
So much agility, desire, and feverish care,
As bicyclists and harpsichordists prove
Who only by moving can balance,
Only by balancing move.

MICHAEL DONAGHY

Man and Wife

Tamed by *Miltown*, we lie on Mother's bed;
the rising sun in war paint dyes us red;
in broad daylight her gilded bed-posts shine,
abandoned, almost Dionysian.
At last the trees are green on Marlborough Street,
blossoms on our magnolia ignite
the morning with their murderous five days' white.
All night I've held your hand,
as if you had
a fourth time faced the kingdom of the mad –
its hackneyed speech, its homicidal eye –
and dragged me home alive . . . Oh my Petite,
clearest of all God's creatures, still all air and nerve:
you were in your twenties, and I,
once hand on glass
and heart in mouth,
outdrank the Rhavs in the heat
of Greenwich Village, fainting at your feet –
too boiled and shy
and poker-faced to make a pass,
while the shrill verve
of your invective scorched the traditional South.

Now twelve years later, you turn your back.
Sleepless, you hold
your pillow to your hollows like a child,

your old-fashioned tirade –
loving, rapid, merciless –
breaks like the Atlantic Ocean on my head.

ROBERT LOWELL

A Marriage

We met
   under a shower
of bird-notes.
   Fifty years passed,
love's moment
   in a world in
servitude to time.
   She was young;
I kissed with my eyes
   closed and opened
them on her wrinkles.
   'Come' said death,
choosing her as his
   partner for
the last dance. And she,
   who in life
had done everything
   with a bird's grace,
opened her bill now
   for the shedding
of one sigh no
   heavier than a feather.

R. S. THOMAS

Meeting at Night

The grey sea and the long black land;
And the yellow half-moon large and low;
And the startled little waves that leap
In fiery ringlets from their sleep,
As I gain the cove with pushing prow,
And quench its speed i' the slushy sand.

Then a mile of warm sea-scented beach;
Three fields to cross till a farm appears;
A tap at the pane, the quick sharp scratch
And blue spurt of a lighted match,
And a voice less loud, thro' its joys and fears,
Than the two hearts beating each to each!

ROBERT BROWNING

Meeting Point

Time was away and somewhere else,
There were two glasses and two chairs
And two people with the one pulse
(Somebody stopped the moving stairs):
Time was away and somewhere else.

And they were neither up nor down;
The stream's music did not stop
Flowing through heather, limpid brown,
Although they sat in a coffee shop
And they were neither up nor down.

The bell was silent in the air
Holding its inverted poise –
Between the clang and clang a flower,
A brazen calyx of no noise:
The bell was silent in the air.

The camels crossed the miles of sand
That stretched around the cups and plates;
The desert was their own, they planned
To portion out the stars and dates:
The camels crossed the miles of sand.

Time was away and somewhere else.
The waiter did not come, the clock
Forgot them and the radio waltz
Came out like water from a rock:
Time was away and somewhere else.

Her fingers flicked away the ash
That bloomed again in tropic trees:
Not caring if the markets crash
When they had forests such as these,
Her fingers flicked away the ash.

God or whatever means the Good
Be praised that time can stop like this,
That what the heart has understood
Can verify in the body's peace
God or whatever means the Good.

Time was away and she was here
And life no longer what it was,
The bell was silent in the air
And all the room one glow because
Time was away and she was here.

LOUIS MACNEICE

Modern Love

It is summer, and we are in a house
That is not ours, sitting at a table
Enjoying minutes of a rented silence,
The upstairs people gone. The pigeons lull
To sleep the under-tens and invalids,
The tree shakes out its shadows to the grass,
The roses rove through the wilds of my neglect,
Our lives flap, and we have no hope of better
Happiness than this, not much to show for love
But how we are, or how this evening is,
Unpeopled, silent, and where we are alive
In a domestic love, seemingly alone,
All other lives worn down to trees and sunlight,
Looking forward to a visit from the cat.

DOUGLAS DUNN

Muse

When I kiss you in all the folding places
of your body, you make that noise like a dog
dreaming, dreaming of the long runs he makes
in answer to some jolt to his hormones,
running across landfills, running, running
by tips and shorelines from the scent of too much,
but still going with head up and snout
in the air because he loves it all
and has to get away. I have to kiss deeper
and more slowly – your neck, your inner arm,
the neat creases under your toes, the shadow
behind your knee, the white angles of your groin –
until you fall quiet because only then
can I get the damned words to come into my mouth.

JO SHAPCOTT

My Last Duchess

That's my last Duchess painted on the wall,
Looking as if she were alive. I call
That piece a wonder, now: Frà Pandolf's hands
Worked busily a day, and there she stands.
Will't please you sit and look at her? I said
'Frà Pandolf' by design, for never read
Strangers like you that pictured countenance,
The depth and passion of its earnest glance,
But to myself they turned (since none puts by
The curtain I have drawn for you, but I)
And seemed as they would ask me, if they durst,
How such a glance came there; so, not the first
Are you to turn and ask thus. Sir, 't was not
Her husband's presence only, called that spot
Of joy into the Duchess' cheek: perhaps
Frà Pandolf chanced to say 'Her mantle laps
Over my lady's wrist too much,' or 'Paint
Must never hope to reproduce the faint
Half-flush that dies along her throat:' such stuff
Was courtesy, she thought, and cause enough
For calling up that spot of joy. She had
A heart – how shall I say? – too soon made glad,
Too easily impressed; she liked whate'er
She looked on, and her looks went everywhere.
Sir, 't was all one! My favour at her breast,
The dropping of the daylight in the West,
The bough of cherries some officious fool
Broke in the orchard for her, the white mule

She rode with round the terrace – all and each
Would draw from her alike the approving speech,
Or blush, at least. She thanked men, – good! but thanked
Somehow – I know not how – as if she ranked
My gift of a nine-hundred-years-old name
With anybody's gift. Who'd stoop to blame
This sort of trifling? Even had you skill
In speech – (which I have not) – to make your will
Quite clear to such an one, and say, 'Just this
Or that in you disgusts me; here you miss,
Or there exceed the mark' – and if she let
Herself be lessoned so, nor plainly set
Her wits to yours, forsooth, and made excuse,
– E'en then would be some stooping; and I choose
Never to stoop. Oh sir, she smiled, no doubt,
Whene'er I passed her, but who passed without
Much the same smile? This grew; I gave commands;
Then all smiles stopped together. There she stands
As if alive. Will't please you rise? We'll meet
The company below, then. I repeat,
The Count your master's known munificence
Is ample warrant that no just pretence
Of mine for dowry will be disallowed;
Though his fair daughter's self, as I avowed
At starting, is my object. Nay, we'll go
Together down, sir. Notice Neptune, though,
Taming a sea-horse, thought a rarity,
Which Claus of Innsbruck cast in bronze for me!

ROBERT BROWNING

My Luve is like a Red, Red Rose

My luve is like a red, red rose,
   That's newly sprung in June:
My luve is like the melodie,
   That's sweetly play'd in tune.
As fair art thou, my bonie lass,
   So deep in luve am I,
And I will luve thee still, my dear,
   Till a' the seas gang dry.

Till a' the seas gang dry, my dear,
   And the rocks melt wi' the sun!
And I will luve thee still, my dear,
   While the sands o' life shall run.
And fare-thee-weel, my only luve,
   And fare-thee-weel a while!
And I will come again, my luve,
   Tho' it were ten-thousand mile.

ROBERT BURNS

'My mistress' eyes are nothing like the sun'

My mistress' eyes are nothing like the sun;
Coral is far more red than her lips' red:
If snow be white, why then her breasts are dun;
If hairs be wires, black wires grow on her head.
I have seen roses damasked, red and white,
But no such roses see I in her cheeks;
And in some perfumes is there more delight
Then in the breath that from my mistress reeks.
I love to hear her speak, yet well I know
That music hath a far more pleasing sound;
I grant I never saw a goddess go;
My mistress, when she walks, treads on the ground.
  And yet, by heaven, I think my love as rare
  As any she belied with false compare.

WILLIAM SHAKESPEARE

My Young Man's a Cornishman

My young man's a Cornishman
He lives in Camborne town,
I met him going up the hill
As I was coming down.

His eye is bright as Dolcoath tin,
His body as china clay,
His hair is dark as Werrington Wood
Upon St Thomas's Day.

He plays the rugby football game
On Saturday afternoon,
And we shall walk on Wilsey Down
Under the bouncing moon.

My young man's a Cornishman,
Won't leave me in the lurch,
And one day we shall married be
Up to Trura church.

He's bought me a ring of Cornish gold,
A belt of copper made,
At Bodmin Fair for my wedding-dress
A purse of silver paid.

And I shall give him scalded cream
And starry-gazy pie,
And make him a saffron cake for tea
And a pasty for by and by.

My young man's a Cornishman,
A proper young man is he,
And a Cornish man with a Cornish maid
Is how it belongs to be.

CHARLES CAUSLEY

Non Sum Qualis Eram Bonae
Sub Regno Cynarae

Last night, ah, yesternight, betwixt her lips and mine
There fell thy shadow, Cynara! thy breath was shed
Upon my soul between the kisses and the wine;
And I was desolate and sick of an old passion,
    Yea, I was desolate and bowed my head:
I have been faithful to thee, Cynara! in my fashion.

All night upon mine heart I felt her warm heart beat,
Night-long within mine arms in love and sleep she lay;
Surely the kisses of her bought red mouth were sweet;
But I was desolate and sick of an old passion,
    When I awoke and found the dawn was gray:
I have been faithful to thee, Cynara! in my fashion.

I have forgot much, Cynara! Gone with the wind,
Flung roses, roses riotously with the throng,
Dancing, to put thy pale, lost lilies out of mind;
But I was desolate and sick of an old passion,
    Yea, all the time, because the dance was long:
I have been faithful to thee, Cynara! in my fashion.

I cried for madder music and for stronger wine,
But when the feast is finished and the lamps expire,
Then falls thy shadow, Cynara! the night is thine;
And I am desolate and sick of an old passion,
    Yea hungry for the lips of my desire:
I have been faithful to thee, Cynara! in my fashion.

ERNEST DOWSON

Not Love Perhaps

This is not Love perhaps – Love that lays down
Its life, that many waters cannot quench, nor the floods
   drown –
But something written in lighter ink, said in a lower tone:
Something perhaps especially our own:
A need at times to be together and talk –
And then the finding we can walk
More firmly through dark narrow places
And meet more easily nightmare faces:
A need to reach out sometimes hand to hand –
And then find Earth less like an alien land:
A need for alliance to defeat
The whisperers at the corner of the street:
A need for inns on roads, islands in seas, halts for
   discoveries to be shared,
Maps checked and notes compared:
A need at times of each for each
Direct as the need of throat and tongue for speech.

A. S. J. TESSIMOND

'Now sleeps the crimson petal, now the white'

Now sleeps the crimson petal, now the white;
Nor waves the cypress in the palace walk;
Nor winks the gold fin in the porphyry font:
The fire-fly wakens: waken thou with me.

Now droops the milkwhite peacock like a ghost,
And like a ghost she glimmers on to me.

Now lies the Earth all Danaë to the stars,
And all thy heart lies open unto me.

Now slides the silent meteor on, and leaves
A shining furrow, as thy thoughts in me.

Now folds the lily all her sweetness up,
And slips into the bosom of the lake:
So fold thyself, my dearest, thou, and slip
Into my bosom and be lost in me.

ALFRED, LORD TENNYSON

'Oh, oh, you will be sorry for that word!'

Oh, oh, you will be sorry for that word!
Give back my book and take my kiss instead.
Was it my enemy or my friend I heard,
'What a big book for such a little head!'
Come, I will show you now my newest hat,
And you may watch me purse my mouth and prink!
Oh, I shall love you still, and all of that.
I never again shall tell you what I think.
I shall be sweet and crafty, soft and sly;
You will not catch me reading any more:
I shall be called a wife to pattern by;
And some day when you knock and push the door,
Some sane day, not too bright and not too stormy,
I shall be gone, and you may whistle for me.

EDNA ST VINCENT MILLAY

One Perfect Rose

A single flow'r he sent me, since we met.
All tenderly his messenger he chose;
Deep-hearted, pure, with scented dew still wet –
One perfect rose.

I knew the language of the floweret;
'My fragile leaves,' it said, 'his heart enclose.'
Love long has taken for his amulet
One perfect rose.

Why is it no one ever sent me yet
One perfect limousine, do you suppose?
Ah no, it's always just my luck to get
One perfect rose.

DOROTHY PARKER

The Otter

When you plunged
The light of Tuscany wavered
And swung through the pool
From top to bottom.

I loved your wet head and smashing crawl,
Your fine swimmer's back and shoulders
Surfacing and surfacing again
This year and every year since.

I sat dry-throated on the warm stones.
You were beyond me.
The mellowed clarities, the grape-deep air
Thinned and disappointed.

Thank God for the slow loadening,
When I hold you now
We are close and deep
As the atmosphere on water.

My two hands are plumbed water.
You are my palpable, lithe
Otter of memory
In the pool of the moment,

Turning to swim on your back,
Each silent, thigh-shaking kick
Re-tilting the light,
Heaving the cool at your neck.

And suddenly you're out,
Back again, intent as ever,
Heavy and frisky in your freshened pelt,
Printing the stones.

SEAMUS HEANEY

Packing Up

Your smell still on me, I delay washing.
Exhausted from having spent
Half the night trying to extort
Commitment from you where none is possible
I stack another room of books
Inside three tea-chests and nail them shut.
I wish words mattered less to me.

MICHAEL FRIED

The Passionate Shepherd to His Love

Come live with me, and be my love,
And we will all the pleasures prove,
That Valleys, groves, hills and fields,
Woods, or steepy mountain yields.

And we will sit upon the Rocks,
Seeing the Shepherds feed their flocks,
By shallow Rivers, to whose falls
Melodious birds sings Madrigals.

And I will make thee beds of Roses
And a thousand fragrant posies,
A cap of flowers, and a kirtle
Embroidered all with leaves of Myrtle;

A gown made of the finest wool
Which from our pretty Lambs we pull;
Fair lined slippers for the cold,
With buckles of the purest gold;

A belt of straw, and Ivy buds,
With Coral clasps and Amber studs,
And if these pleasures may thee move,
Come live with me, and be my love.

The Shepherds' Swains shall dance and sing
For thy delight each May-morning:
If these delights thy mind may move;
Then live with me, and be my love.

CHRISTOPHER MARLOWE

Perfect Day

I am just a woman of the shore
wearing your coat against the snow
that falls on the oyster-catchers' tracks
and on our own; falls
on the still grey waters
of Loch Morar, and on our shoulders
gentle as restraint: a perfect weight
of snow as tree-boughs
and fences bear against a loaded sky:
one flake more, they'd break.

KATHLEEN JAMIE

Porphyria's Lover

The rain set early in tonight,
  The sullen wind was soon awake,
It tore the elm-tops down for spite,
  And did its worst to vex the lake:
  I listened with heart fit to break.
When glided in Porphyria; straight
  She shut the cold out and the storm,
And kneeled and made the cheerless grate
  Blaze up, and all the cottage warm;
  Which done, she rose, and from her form
Withdrew the dripping cloak and shawl,
  And laid her soiled gloves by, untied
Her hat and let the damp hair fall,
  And, last, she sat down by my side
  And called me. When no voice replied,
She put my arm about her waist,
  And made her smooth white shoulder bare,
And all her yellow hair displaced,
  And, stooping, made my cheek lie there,
  And spread, o'er all, her yellow hair,
Murmuring how she loved me – she
  Too weak, for all her heart's endeavour,
To set its struggling passion free
  From pride, and vainer ties dissever,
  And give herself to me for ever.
But passion sometimes would prevail,
  Nor could to-night's gay feast restrain
A sudden thought of one so pale
  For love of her, and all in vain:

So, she was come through wind and rain.
Be sure I looked up at her eyes
   Happy and proud; at last I knew
Porphyria worshipped me; surprise
   Made my heart swell, and still it grew
   While I debated what to do.
That moment she was mine, mine, fair,
   Perfectly pure and good: I found
A thing to do, and all her hair
   In one long yellow string I wound
   Three times her little throat around,
And strangled her. No pain felt she;
   I am quite sure she felt no pain.
As a shut bud that holds a bee,
   I warily oped her lids: again
   Laughed the blue eyes without a stain.
And I untightened next the tress
   About her neck; her cheek once more
Blushed bright beneath my burning kiss:
   I propped her head up as before,
   Only, this time my shoulder bore
Her head, which droops upon it still:
   The smiling rosy little head,
So glad it has its utmost will,
   That all it scorned at once is fled,
   And I, its love, am gained instead!
Porphyria's love: she guessed not how
   Her darling one wish would be heard.
And thus we sit together now,
   And all night long we have not stirred,
   And yet God has not said a word!

ROBERT BROWNING

Recuerdo

We were very tired, we were very merry –
We had gone back and forth all night on the ferry.
It was bare and bright, and smelled like a stable –
But we looked into a fire, we leaned across a table,
We lay on a hill-top underneath the moon;
And the whistles kept blowing, and the dawn came soon.

We were very tired, we were very merry –
We had gone back and forth all night on the ferry;
And you ate an apple, and I ate a pear,
From a dozen of each we had bought somewhere;
And the sky went wan, and the wind came cold,
And the sun rose dripping, a bucketful of gold.

We were very tired, we were very merry,
We had gone back and forth all night on the ferry.
We hailed, 'Good morrow, mother!' to a shawl-covered
        head,
And bought a morning paper, which neither of us read;
And she wept, 'God bless you!' for the apples and pears,
And we gave her all our money but our subway fares.

EDNA ST VINCENT MILLAY

Remember This

You won't remember this, but I will:
A gradually tightening avenue of trees
And where it locks
What seems from here the most yearningly delicate
Intrusion of white leaves
May yet blacken the unclouded pool of sun
That summons you.
Keep going
Even though I mean to stay; keep going
Even though I can't any more imagine
What I'll find most hard to bear
On the way back from here,
On the way home
To where we first vowed we'd try again to say:
You won't remember this.

IAN HAMILTON

Re-reading Katherine Mansfield's
Bliss and Other Stories

A pressed fly, like a skeleton of gauze,
Has waited here between page 98
And 99, in the story called 'Bliss',
Since the summer of '62, its date,

It's last day in a trap of pages. Prose
Fly, what can 'Je ne parle pas français' mean
To you who died in Scotland, when I closed
These two sweet pages you were crushed between?

Here is a green bus ticket for a week
In May, my place mark in 'The Dill Pickle'.
I did not come home that Friday. I flick
Through all our years, my love, and I love you still.

These stories must have been inside my head
That day, falling in love, preparing this
Good life; and this, this fly, verbosely buried
In 'Bliss', one dry tear punctuating 'Bliss'.

DOUGLAS DUNN

The Ring

He has married me with a ring, a ring of bright water
Whose ripples travel from the heart of the sea,
He has married me with a ring of light, the glitter
Broadcast on the swift river.
He has married me with the sun's circle
Too dazzling to see, traced in summer sky.
He has crowned me with the wreath of white cloud
That gathers on the snowy summit of the mountain,
Ringed me round with the world-circling wind,
Bound me to the whirlwind's centre.
He has married me with the orbit of the moon
And with the boundless circle of the stars,
With the orbits that measure years, months, days and
    nights,
Set the tides flowing,
Command the winds to travel or be at rest.

At the ring's centre,
Spirit, or angel troubling the still pool,
Causality not in nature,
Finger's touch that summons at a point, a moment
Stars and planets, life and light
Or gathers cloud about an apex of cold,
Transcendent touch of love summons my world to being.

KATHLEEN RAINE

Rondeau Redoublé

There are so many kinds of awful men –
One can't avoid them all. She often said
She'd never make the same mistake again:
She always made a new mistake instead.

The chinless type who made her feel ill-bred;
The practised charmer, less than charming when
He talked about the wife and kids and fled –
There are so many kinds of awful men.

The half-crazed hippy, deeply into Zen,
Whose cryptic homilies she came to dread;
The fervent youth who worshipped Tony Benn –
'One can't avoid them all,' she often said.

The ageing banker, rich and overfed,
Who held forth on the dollar and the yen –
Though there were many more mistakes ahead,
She'd never make the same mistake again.

The budding poet, scribbling in his den
Odes not to her but to his pussy, Fred;
The drunk who fell asleep at nine or ten –
She always made a new mistake instead.

And so the gambler was at least unwed
And didn't preach or sneer or wield a pen

Or hoard his wealth or take the Scotch to bed.
She'd lived and learned and lived and learned but then
There are so many kinds.

WENDY COPE

Sex and the Over Forties

It's too good for them,
they look so unattractive undressed –
let them read paperbacks!

A few things to keep in readiness –
a flensing knife, a ceiling mirror,
a cassette of *The Broken Heart*.

More luncheons than lust,
more meetings on Northern Line stations,
more discussions of children's careers.

A postcard from years back
I'm twenty-one, in Italy and in love!
Wagner wrote *Tristan* at forty-four.

Trying it with noises and in strange positions,
trying it with the young themselves,
trying to keep it up with the Joneses!

All words and no play,
all animals fleeing a forest fire,
all Apollo's grafters running.

Back to the dream in the garden,
back to the pictures in the drawer,
back to back, tonight and every night.

PETER PORTER

'Shall I compare thee to a summer's day?'

Shall I compare thee to a summer's day?
Thou art more lovely and more temperate.
Rough winds do shake the darling buds of May,
And summer's lease hath all too short a date.
Sometimes too hot the eye of heaven shines,
And often is his gold complexion dimmed;
And every fair from fair sometimes declines,
By chance or nature's changing course untrimmed.
But thy eternal summer shall not fade,
Nor lose possession of that fair thou ow'st,
Nor shall Death brag thou wand'rest in his shade,
When in eternal lines to time thou grow'st,
  So long as men can breathe or eyes can see,
  So long lives this, and this gives life to thee.

WILLIAM SHAKESPEARE

She Moved Through the Fair

My young love said to me, 'My brothers won't mind,
And my parents won't slight you for your lack of kind.'
Then she stepped away from me, and this she did say
'It will not be long, love, till our wedding day.'

She stepped away from me and she moved through the fair,
And fondly I watched her go here and go there,
Then she went her way homeward with one star awake,
As the swan in the evening moves over the lake.

The people were saying no two were ere wed
But one had a sorrow that never was said,
And I smiled as she passed with her goods and her gear,
And that was the last that I saw of my dear.

I dreamt it last night that my young love came in,
So softly she entered, her feet made no din;
She came close beside me, and this she did say
'It will not be long, love, till our wedding day.'

PADRAIC COLUM

She Walks in Beauty, like the Night

She walks in Beauty, like the night
   Of cloudless climes and starry skies;
And all that's best of dark and bright
   Meet in her aspect and her eyes:
Thus mellowed to that tender light
   Which Heaven to gaudy day denies.

One shade the more, one ray the less,
   Had half impaired the nameless grace
Which waves in every raven tress,
   Or softly lightens o'er her face;
Where thoughts serenely sweet express,
   How pure, how dear their dwelling-place.

And on that cheek, and o'er that brow,
   So soft, so calm, yet eloquent,
The smiles that win, the tints that glow,
   But tell of days in goodness spent,
A mind at peace with all below,
   A heart whose love is innocent!

LORD BYRON

The Silken Tent

She is as in a field a silken tent
At midday when a sunny summer breeze
Has dried the dew and all its ropes relent,
So that in guys it gently sways at ease,
And its supporting central cedar pole,
That is its pinnacle to heavenward
And signifies the sureness of the soul,
Seems to owe naught to any single cord,
But strictly held by none, is loosely bound
By countless silken ties of love and thought
To everything on earth the compass round,
And only by one's going slightly taut
In the capriciousness of summer air
Is of the slightest bondage made aware.

ROBERT FROST

'Since there's no help, come, let us kiss and part'

Since there's no help, come, let us kiss and part –
Nay, I have done: you get no more of me;
And I am glad, yea, glad with all my heart
That thus so cleanly I myself can free.
Shake hands forever, cancel all our vows,
And when we meet at any time again,
Be it not seen in either of our brows
That we one jot of former love retain.
Now at the last gasp of love's latest breath,
When, his pulse failing, Passion speechless lies,
When Faith is kneeling by his bed of death,
And Innocence is closing up his eyes, –
Now, if thou wouldst, when all have given him over,
From death to life thou mightst him yet recover.

MICHAEL DRAYTON

Skin Full

I laugh till my jaw unhinges,
we hold me in with ribboning fingers.
Moderation in moderation. Who said that?
It makes extraordinary sense to me.

You say that life is a three-legged race.
They show us the door and we have some difficulty,
bound like that from thigh to ankle.
The street is a blanket. We will sleep

with you on your front, me on your back.
The night will be endless and we will be endless,
layer on layer, infinitely warm.
I sing as we lie shoulder to shoulder

and tell you there is no such thing as anything
that is not a small circle. Now it is morning.
Can the bones we broke out of be mended?
My eyes . . . The sun picks over their embers.

LAVINIA GREENLAW

The Skunk

Up, black, striped and damasked like the chasuble
At a funeral mass, the skunk's tail
Paraded the skunk. Night after night
I expected her like a visitor.

The refrigerator whinnied into silence.
My desk light softened beyond the veranda.
Small oranges loomed in the orange tree.
I began to be tense as a voyeur.

After eleven years I was composing
Love-letters again, broaching the word 'wife'
Like a stored cask, as if its slender vowel
Had mutated into the night earth and air

Of California. The beautiful, useless
Tang of eucalyptus spelt your absence.
The aftermath of a mouthful of wine
Was like inhaling you off a cold pillow.

And there she was, the intent and glamorous,
Ordinary, mysterious skunk,
Mythologized, demythologized,
Snuffing the boards five feet beyond me.

It all came back to me last night, stirred
By the sootfall of your things at bedtime,
Your head-down, tail-up hunt in a bottom drawer
For the black plunge-line nightdress.

SEAMUS HEANEY

A Slice of Wedding Cake

Why have such scores of lovely, gifted girls
   Married impossible men?
Simple self-sacrifice may be ruled out,
   And missionary endeavour, nine times out of ten.

Repeat 'impossible men': not merely rustic,
   Foul-tempered or depraved
(Dramatic foils chosen to show the world
   How well women behave, and always have behaved).

Impossible men: idle, illiterate,
   Self-pitying, dirty, sly,
For whose appearance even in City parks
   Excuses must be made to casual passers-by.

Has God's supply of tolerable husbands
   Fallen, in fact, so low?
Or do I always over-value woman
   At the expense of man?
     Do I?
      It might be so.

ROBERT GRAVES

'So, we'll go no more a-roving'

So, we'll go no more a-roving
    So late into the night,
Though the heart be still as loving,
    And the moon be still as bright.

For the sword outwears its sheath,
    And the soul wears out the breast,
And the heart must pause to breathe,
    And love itself have rest.

Though the night was made for loving,
    And the day returns too soon,
Yet we'll go no more a roving
    By the light of the moon.

LORD BYRON

'somewhere i have never travelled,
gladly beyond'

somewhere i have never travelled,gladly beyond
any experience,your eyes have their silence:
in your most frail gesture are things which enclose me,
or which i cannot touch because they are too near

your slightest look easily will unclose me
though i have closed myself as fingers,
you open always petal by petal myself as Spring opens
(touching skilfully,mysteriously)her first rose

or if your wish be to close me,i and
my life will shut very beautifully,suddenly,
as when the heart of this flower imagines
the snow carefully everywhere descending;

nothing which we are to perceive in this world equals
the power of your intense fragility:whose texture
compels me with the colour of its countries,
rendering death and forever with each breathing

(i do not know what it is about you that closes
and opens;only something in me understands
the voice of your eyes is deeper than all roses)
nobody,not even the rain,has such small hands

E. E. CUMMINGS

A Subaltern's Love-Song

Miss J. Hunter Dunn, Miss J. Hunter Dunn,
Furnish'd and burnish'd by Aldershot sun,
What strenuous singles we played after tea,
We in the tournament – you against me!

Love-thirty, love-forty, oh! weakness of joy,
The speed of a swallow, the grace of a boy,
With carefullest carelessness, gaily you won,
I am weak from your loveliness, Joan Hunter Dunn.

Miss Joan Hunter Dunn, Miss Joan Hunter Dunn,
How mad I am, sad I am, glad that you won.
The warm-handled racket is back in its press,
But my shock-headed victor, she loves me no less.

Her father's euonymus shines as we walk,
And swing past the summer-house, buried in talk,
And cool the verandah that welcomes us in
To the six-o'clock news and a lime-juice and gin.

The scent of the conifers, sound of the bath,
The view from my bedroom of moss-dappled path,
As I struggle with double-end evening tie,
For we dance at the Golf Club, my victor and I.

On the floor of her bedroom lie blazer and shorts
And the cream-coloured walls are be-trophied with sports,
And westering, questioning settles the sun
On your low-leaded window, Miss Joan Hunter Dunn.

The Hillman is waiting, the light's in the hall,
The pictures of Egypt are bright on the wall,
My sweet, I am standing beside the oak stair
And there on the landing's the light on your hair.

By roads 'not adopted', by woodlanded ways,
She drove to the club in the late summer haze,
Into nine-o'clock Camberley, heavy with bells
And mushroomy, pine-woody, evergreen smells.

Miss Joan Hunter Dunn, Miss Joan Hunter Dunn,
I can hear from the car-park the dance has begun.
Oh! full Surrey twilight! importunate band!
Oh! strongly adorable tennis-girl's hand!

Around us are Rovers and Austins afar,
Above us, the intimate roof of the car,
And here on my right is the girl of my choice,
With the tilt of her nose and the chime of her voice,

And the scent of her wrap, and the words never said,
And the ominous, ominous dancing ahead.
We sat in the car park till twenty to one
And now I'm engaged to Miss Joan Hunter Dunn.

JOHN BETJEMAN

Sudden Light

I have been here before,
But when or how I cannot tell:
I know the grass beyond the door,
The sweet keen smell,
The sighing sound, the lights around the shore.

You have been mine before,
How long ago I may not know:
But just when at that swallow's soar
Your neck turned so,
Some veil did fall – I knew it all of yore.

Has this been thus before?
And shall not thus time's eddying flight
Still with our lives our love restore
In death's despite,
And day and night yield one delight once more?

DANTE GABRIEL ROSSETTI

The Sun Rising

Busy old fool, unruly sun,
    Why dost thou thus
Through windows and through curtains call on us?
Must to thy motions lovers' seasons run?
    Saucy pedantic wretch, go chide
    Late schoolboys, and sour prentices;
Go tell court huntsmen that the king will ride;
Call country ants to harvest offices:
Love, all alike, no season knows, nor clime,
Nor hours, days, months, which are the rags of time.

Thy beams, so reverend, and strong
    Why shouldst thou think?
I could eclipse and cloud them with a wink,
But that I would not lose her sight so long:
    If her eyes have not blinded thine,
    Look, and tomorrow late tell me
Whether both th' India's of spice and mine
Be where thou leftst them, or lie here with me.
Ask for those kings whom thou sawst yesterday,
And thou shalt hear, all here in one bed lay.

She's all states, and all princes, I;
    Nothing else is.
Princes do but play us; compared to this,
All honour's mimic; all wealth alchimy.
    Thou, sun, art half as happy as we,
    In that the world's contracted thus;

Thine age asks ease, and since thy duties be
To warm the world, that's done in warming us.
Shine here to us, and thou art everywhere:
This bed thy centre is, these walls, thy sphere.

JOHN DONNE

Talking in Bed

Talking in bed ought to be easiest,
Lying together there goes back so far,
An emblem of two people being honest.

Yet more and more time passes silently.
Outside, the wind's incomplete unrest
Builds and disperses clouds about the sky,

And dark towns heap up on the horizon.
None of this cares for us. Nothing shows why
At this unique distance from isolation

It becomes still more difficult to find
Words at once true and kind,
Or not untrue and not unkind.

PHILIP LARKIN

Tamer and Hawk

I thought I was so tough,
But gentled at your hands,
Cannot be quick enough
To fly for you and show
That when I go I go
At your commands.

Even in flight above
I am no longer free:
You seeled me with your love,
I am blind to other birds –
The habit of your words
Has hooded me.

As formerly, I wheel
I hover and I twist,
But only want the feel,
In my possessive thought,
Of catcher and of caught
Upon your wrist.

You but half civilize,
Taming me in this way.
Through having only eyes
For you I fear to lose,
I lose to keep, and choose
Tamer as prey.

THOM GUNN

'They flee from me that sometime did me seek'

They flee from me that sometime did me seek
   With naked foot stalking in my chamber.
I have seen them gentle tame and meek
   That now are wild and do not remember
   That sometime they put themselves in danger
To take bread at my hand; and now they range
Busily seeking with a continual change.

Thanked be fortune, it hath been otherwise
   Twenty times better; but once in special,
In thin array after a pleasant guise,
   When her loose gown from her shoulders did fall,
   And she me caught in her arms long and small;
And therewithal sweetly did me kiss,
And softly said, *Dear heart, how like you this?*

It was no dream: I lay broad waking.
   But all is turned thorough my gentleness
Into a strange fashion of forsaking;
   And I have leave to go of her goodness
   And she also to use newfangleness.
But since that I so kindly am served,
I would fain know what she hath deserved.

THOMAS WYATT

To Althea, from Prison

When love with unconfinèd wings
   Hovers within my gates,
And my divine Althea brings
   To whisper at the grates;
When I lie tangled in her hair,
   And fettered to her eye,
The gods that wanton in the air
   Know no such liberty.

When flowing cups run swiftly round,
   With no allaying Thames,
Our careless heads with roses bound,
   Our hearts with loyal flames;
When thirsty grief in wine we steep,
   When healths and draughts go free,
Fishes that tipple in the deep
   Know no such liberty.

When, like committed linnets, I
   With shriller throat shall sing
The sweetness, mercy, majesty
   And glories of my king;
When I shall voice aloud how good
   He is, how great should be;
Enlargèd winds that curl the flood
   Know no such Liberty.

Stone walls do not a prison make,
   Nor iron bars a cage;
Minds innocent and quiet take
   That for an hermitage:
If I have freedom in my love,
   And in my soul am free,
Angels alone that sore above
   Enjoy such liberty.

RICHARD LOVELACE

To His Coy Mistress

Had we but world enough, and time,
This coyness, Lady, were no crime.
We would sit down, and think which way
To walk, and pass our long love's day.
Thou by the Indian Ganges' side
Shouldst rubies find: I by the tide
Of Humber would complain. I would
Love you ten years before the Flood:
And you should, if you please, refuse
Till the conversion of the Jews.
My vegetable love should grow
Vaster then empires, and more slow.
An hundred years should go to praise
Thine eyes, and on thy forehead gaze.
Two hundred to adore each breast;
But thirty thousand to the rest.
An age at least to every part,
And the last age should show your heart:
For, Lady, you deserve this state;
Nor would I love at lower rate.
   But at my back I always hear
Time's wingèd chariot hurrying near;
And yonder all before us lie
Deserts of vast eternity.
Thy beauty shall no more be found;
Nor, in thy marble vault, shall sound
My echoing song: then worms shall try
That long-preserved virginity:

And your quaint honour turn to dust;
And into ashes all my lust.
The grave's a fine and private place,
But none, I think, do there embrace.
    Now therefore, while the youthful glue
Sits on thy skin like morning dew,
And while thy willing soul transpires
At every pore with instant fires,
Now let us sport us while we may;
And now, like amorous birds of prey,
Rather at once our time devour
Than languish in his slow-chapped power.
Let us roll all our strength, and all
Our sweetness, up into one ball:
And tear our pleasures with rough strife
Through the iron gates of life.
Thus, though we cannot make our sun
Stand still, yet we will make him run.

ANDREW MARVELL

To His Lost Lover

Now they are no longer
any trouble to each other

he can turn things over, get down to that list
of things that never happened, all of the lost

unfinishable business.
For instance . . . for instance,

how he never clipped and kept her hair, or drew a hairbrush
through that style of hers, and never knew how not to blush

at the fall of her name in close company.
How they never slept like buried cutlery –

two spoons or forks cupped perfectly together,
or made the most of some heavy weather –

walked out into hard rain under sheet lightning,
or did the gears while the other was driving.

How he never raised his fingertips
to stop the segments of her lips

from breaking the news,
or tasted the fruit,

or picked for himself the pear of her heart,
or lifted her hand to where his own heart

was a small, dark, terrified bird
in her grip. Where it hurt.

Or said the right thing,
or put it in writing.

And never fled the black mile back to his house
before midnight, or coaxed another button of her blouse,

then another,
or knew her

favourite colour,
her taste, her flavour,

and never ran a bath or held a towel for her,
or soft-soaped her, or whipped her hair

into an ice-cream cornet or a beehive
of lather, or acted out of turn, or misbehaved

when he might have, or worked a comb
where no comb had been, or walked back home

through a black mile hugging a punctured heart,
where it hurt, where it hurt, or helped her hand

to his butterfly heart
in its two blue halves.

And never almost cried,
and never once described

an attack of the heart,
or under a silk shirt

nursed in his hand her breast,
her left, like a tear of flesh

wept by the heart,
where it hurts,

or brushed with his thumb the nut of her nipple,
or drank intoxicating liquors from her navel.

Or christened the Pole Star in her name,
or shielded the mask of her face like a flame,

a pilot light,
or stayed the night,

or steered her back to that house of his,
or said 'Don't ask me to say how it is

I like you.
I just might do.'

How he never figured out a fireproof plan,
or unravelled her hand, as if her hand

were a solid ball
of silver foil

and discovered a lifeline hiding inside it,
and measured the trace of his own alongside it.

But said some things and never meant them –
sweet nothings anybody could have mentioned.

And left unsaid some things he should have spoken,
about the heart, where it hurt exactly, and how often.

SIMON ARMITAGE

To My Wife at Midnight

Are you to say goodnight
And turn away under
The blanket of your delight?

Are you to let me go
Alone to sleep beside you
Into the drifting snow?

Where we each reach,
Sleeping alone together,
Nobody can touch.

Is the cat's window open?
Shall I turn into your back?
And what is to happen?

What is to happen to us
And what is to happen to each
Of us asleep in our places?

II

I mean us both going
Into sleep at our ages
To sleep and get our fairing.

They have all gone home.
Night beasts are coming out.
The black wood of Madron

Is just waking up.
I hear the rain outside
To help me to go to sleep.

Nessie, don't let my soul
Skip and miss a beat
And cause me to fall.

III

Are you asleep I say
Into the back of your neck
For you not to hear me.

Are you asleep? I hear
Your heart under the pillow
Saying my dear my dear

My dear for all it's worth.
Where is the dun's moor
Which began your breath?

IV

Ness, to tell you the truth
I am drifting away
Down to fish for the saithe.

Is the cat's window open?
The weather is on my shoulder
And I am drifting down

Into O can you hear me
Among your Dunsmuir Clan?
Are you coming out to play?

V

Did I behave badly
On the field at Culloden?
I lie sore-wounded now

By all activities, and
The terrible acts of my time
Are only a distant sound.

With responsibility
I am drifting off
Breathing regularly

Into my younger days
To play the games of Greenock
Beside the sugar-house quays.

VI

Nessie Dunsmuir, I say
Wheesht wheesht to myself
To help me now to go

Under into somewhere
In the redcoat rain.
Buckle me for the war.

Are you to say goodnight
And kiss me and fasten
My drowsy armour tight?

My dear camp-follower,
Hap the blanket round me
And tuck in a flower.

Maybe from my sleep
In the stoure at Culloden
I'll see you here asleep

In your lonely place.

W. S. GRAHAM

The Train

How like a man to choose a crowded train
To say that we must never meet again!
Or was it masculine low cunning
So that I could not make a scene?
It might have been.

O anguish as the suburbs clattered by!
We had to shout to make our voices heard,
But still I understood each telling word –
'We can't go on like this,
I thought you understood;
You must see it's no good.'

Like statues we were standing in the corridor
And people, pushing past with cases
Glared at us both for being in the way,
And I said all the bitter things
I had not meant to say.

I put dark glasses on to hide my eyes,
But then I could not see your face
To see if I had hurt you
But I hoped I had.
Oh, I behaved with little grace.

And still you stood there, silent and unbending.
God! What an ending!

MARY WILSON

[163]

True Love

In the middle of the night, when we get up
after making love, we look at each other
in total friendship, we know so fully
what the other has been doing. Bound to each other like
soldiers coming out of a battle,
bound with the tie of the birth-room, we
wander down the hall to the bathroom, I can
hardly walk, we weave through the dark
soft air, I know where you are
with my eyes closed, we are bound to each other with the
huge invisible threads of sex, though our
sexes themselves are muted, dark and
exhausted and delicately crushed, the whole
body is a sex – surely this
is the most blessed time of life,
the children deep asleep in their beds like a
vein of coal and a vein of gold
not discovered yet. I sit on the
toilet in the dark, you are somewhere in the room, I
open the window and the snow has fallen in a
deep drift against the pane, I
look up into it, a
world of cold crystals, silent and
glistening so I call out to you and you
come and hold my hand and I say
I cannot see beyond it! I cannot see beyond it!

SHARON OLDS

Tryst

Night slips, trailing behind it
a suddenly innocent darkness.
Am I safe, now, to slip home?

My fists tighten your collar, your fingers
lock in my hair and we hover
between discretion and advertised purpose.

Dawn traffic in both directions,
taxis, milk floats, builders' vans.
Each proposes a service or poses a threat

like the police, slumped couples in cars
left to patrol each other, to converge
at a red light that stops little else.

Each separation is outweighed
by more faith, more sadness;
accumulated static, the shock in every step.

I go to sleep where my life is sleeping
and wake late to a fused morning,
a blistered mouth.

LAVINIA GREENLAW

Two Cures for Love

1. Don't see him. Don't phone or write a letter.
2. The easy way: get to know him better.

WENDY COPE

A Valediction Forbidding Mourning

As virtuous men pass mildly away,
    And whisper to the souls, to go,
Whilst some of their sad friends do say,
    The breath goes now, and some say, no:

So let us melt, and make no noise,
    No tear-floods, nor sigh-tempests move,
'Twere prophanation of our joys
    To tell the laity our love.

Moving of th'earth brings harms and fears,
    Men reckon what it did and meant,
But trepidation of the spheres,
    Though greater far, is innocent.

Dull sublunary lovers love
    (Whose soul is sense) cannot admit
Absence, because it doth remove
    Those things which elemented it.

But we by a love, so much refin'd,
    That our selves know not what it is,
Inter-assured of the mind,
    Care less, eyes, lips, and hands to miss.

Our two souls therefore, which are one,
    Though I must go, endure not yet
A breach, but an expansion,
    Like gold to airy thinness beat.

If they be two, they are two so
  As stiff twin compasses are two,
Thy soul the fixt foot, makes no show
  To move, but doth, if th'other do.

And though it in the center sit,
  Yet when the other far doth roam,
It leans, and harkens after it,
  And grows erect, as that comes home.

Such wilt thou be to me, who must
  Like th'other foot, obliquely run.
Thy firmness makes my circle just,
  And makes me end, where I begun.

JOHN DONNE

Valentine

Not a red rose or a satin heart.

I give you an onion.
It is a moon wrapped in brown paper.
It promises light
like the careful undressing of love.

Here.
It will blind you with tears
like a lover.
It will make your reflection
a wobbling photo of grief.

I am trying to be truthful.

Not a cute card or a kissogram.

I give you an onion.
Its fierce kiss will stay on your lips,
possessive and faithful
as we are,
for as long as we are.

Take it.
Its platinum loops shrink to a wedding-ring,
if you like.
Lethal.
Its scent will cling to your fingers,
cling to your knife.

CAROL ANN DUFFY

Valentine

The things about you I appreciate
   May seem indelicate:
I'd like to find you in the shower
And chase the soap for half an hour.
I'd like to have you in my power
   And see your eyes dilate.
I'd like to have your back to scour
And other parts to lubricate.
Sometimes I feel it is my fate
To chase you screaming up a tower
   Or make you cower
By asking you to differentiate
   Nietzsche from Schopenhauer.
I'd like successfully to guess your weight
   And win you at a fête.
I'd like to offer you a flower.

I like the hair upon your shoulders,
Falling like water over boulders.
I like the shoulders, too: they are essential.
Your collar-bones have great potential
(I'd like all your particulars in folders
   Marked *Confidential*).

I like your cheeks, I like your nose,
I like the way your lips disclose
The neat arrangement of your teeth
(Half above and half beneath)
   In rows.

I like your eyes, I like their fringes.
The way they focus on me gives me twinges.
Your upper arms drive me berserk.
I like the way your elbows work,
   On hinges.

I like your wrists, I like your glands,
I like the fingers on your hands.
I'd like to teach them how to count,
And certain things we might exchange,
Something familiar for something strange.
I'd like to give you just the right amount
   And get some change.

I like it when you tilt your cheek up.
I like the way you nod and hold a teacup.
I like your legs when you unwind them.
Even in trousers I don't mind them.
I like each softly-moulded kneecap.
I like the little crease behind them.
I'd always know, without a recap,
   Where to find them.

I like the sculpture of your ears.
I like the way your profile disappears
Whenever you decide to turn and face me.
I'd like to cross two hemispheres
   And have you chase me.
I'd like to smuggle you across frontiers
Or sail with you at night into Tangiers.
   I'd like you to embrace me.

I'd like to see you ironing your skirt
    And cancelling other dates.
I'd like to button up your shirt.
I like the way your chest inflates.
I'd like to soothe you when you're hurt
Or frightened senseless by invertebrates.

I'd like you even if you were malign
And had a yen for sudden homicide.
I'd let you put insecticide
    Into my wine.
I'd even like you if you were the Bride
    Of Frankenstein
Or something ghoulish out of Mamoulian's
    Jekyll and Hyde.
I'd even like you as my Julian
Of Norwich or Cathleen ni Houlihan.
    How melodramatic
If you were something muttering in attics
Like Mrs Rochester or a student of Boolean
    Mathematics.

You are the end of self-abuse.
You are the eternal feminine.
I'd like to find a good excuse
To call on you and find you in.
I'd like to put my hand beneath your chin,
    And see you grin.
I'd like to taste your Charlotte Russe,
I'd like to feel my lips upon your skin,
I'd like to make you reproduce.

I'd like you in my confidence.
I'd like to be your second look.
I'd like to let you try the French Defence
    And mate you with my rook.
I'd like to be your preference
    And hence
I'd like to be around when you unhook.
I'd like to be your only audience,
The final name in your appointment book,
    Your future tense.

JOHN FULLER

Warming Her Pearls

for Judith Radstone

Next to my own skin, her pearls. My mistress
bids me wear them, warm them, until evening
when I'll brush her hair. At six, I place them
round her cool, white throat. All day I think of her,

resting in the Yellow Room, contemplating silk
or taffeta, which gown tonight? She fans herself
whilst I work willingly, my slow heat entering
each pearl. Slack on my neck, her rope.

She's beautiful. I dream about her
in my attic bed; picture her dancing
with tall men, puzzled by my faint, persistent scent
beneath her French perfume, her milky stones.

I dust her shoulders with a rabbit's foot,
watch the soft blush seep through her skin
like an indolent sigh. In her looking-glass
my red lips part as though I want to speak.

Full moon. Her carriage brings her home. I see
her every movement in my head . . . Undressing,
taking off her jewels, her slim hand reaching
for the case, slipping naked into bed, the way

she always does . . . And I lie here awake,
knowing the pearls are cooling even now
in the room where my mistress sleeps. All night
I feel their absence and I burn.

CAROL ANN DUFFY

We Don't Know How to Say Goodbye

We don't know how to say good-bye –
We keep wandering arm in arm.
Twilight has begun to fall,
You are pensive and I keep still.

Let's go into a church – we will watch
A funeral, christenings, a marriage service,
Without looking at each other, we will leave . . .
What's wrong with us?

Or let's sit on the trampled snow
Of the graveyard, sighing lightly,
And with your walking stick you'll outline palaces
Where we will be together always.

ANNA AKHMATOVA

Wedding

From time to time our love is like a sail
and when the sail begins to alternate
from tack to tack, it's like a swallowtail
and when the swallow flies it's like a coat;
and if the coat is yours, it has a tear
like a wide mouth and when the mouth begins
to draw the wind, it's like a trumpeter
and when the trumpet blows, it blows like millions . . .
and this, my love, when millions come and go
beyond the need of us, is like a trick;
and when the trick begins, it's like a toe
tip-toeing on a rope, which is like luck;
and when the luck begins, it's like a wedding,
which is like love, which is like everything.

ALICE OSWALD

Wedding-Wind

The wind blew all my wedding-day,
And my wedding-night was the night of the high wind;
And a stable door was banging, again and again,
That he must go and shut it, leaving me
Stupid in candlelight, hearing rain,
Seeing my face in the twisted candlestick,
Yet seeing nothing. When he came back
He said the horses were restless, and I was sad
That any man or beast that night should lack
The happiness I had.

          Now in the day
All's ravelled under the sun by the wind's blowing.
He has gone to look at the floods, and I
Carry a chipped pail to the chicken-run,
Set it down, and stare. All is the wind
Hunting through clouds and forests, thrashing
My apron and the hanging cloths on the line.
Can it be borne, this bodying-forth by wind
Of joy my actions turn on, like a thread
Carrying beads? Shall I be let to sleep
Now this perpetual morning shares my bed?
Can even death dry up
These new delighted lakes, conclude
Our kneeling as cattle by all-generous waters?

PHILIP LARKIN

Western Wind

Western wind, when will thou blow,
The small rain down can rain?
Christ, if my love were in my arms,
And I in my bed again!

ANON

'What lips my lips have kissed, and where, and why'

What lips my lips have kissed, and where, and why,
I have forgotten, and what arms have lain
Under my head till morning; but the rain
Is full of ghosts tonight, that tap and sigh
Upon the glass and listen for reply,
And in my heart there stirs a quiet pain
For unremembered lads that not again
Will turn to me at midnight with a cry.
Thus in the winter stands the lonely tree,
Nor knows what birds have vanished one by one,
Yet knows its boughs more silent than before:
I cannot say what loves have come and gone,
I only know that summer sang in me
A little while, that in me sings no more.

EDNA ST VINCENT MILLAY

'When in disgrace with Fortune and men's eyes'

When in disgrace with Fortune and men's eyes,
I all alone beweep my outcast state,
And trouble deaf heaven with my bootless cries,
And looke upon my self and curse my fate,
Wishing me like to one more rich in hope,
Featur'd like him, like him with friends possessed,
Desiring this man's art, and that man's scope,
With what I most enjoy contented least,
Yet in these thoughts my self almost despising,
Happily I think on thee, and then my state,
(Like to the Lark at break of day arising)
From sullen earth sings hymns at Heaven's gate,
    For thy sweet love remembered such wealth brings,
    That then I scorn to change my state with Kings.

WILLIAM SHAKESPEARE

'When to the Sessions of sweet silent thought'

When to the Sessions of sweet silent thought,
I summon up remembrance of things past,
I sigh the lack of many a thing I sought,
And with old woes new wail my dear time's waste:
Then can I drown an eye (unus'd to flow)
For precious friends hid in death's dateless night,
And weep a fresh love's long since cancelled woe,
And moan th'expense of many a vanished sight.
Then can I grieve at grievances foregone,
And heavily from woe to woe tell o'er
The sad account of fore-bemoaned moan,
Which I new pay as if not pay'd before.
   But if the while I think on thee (dear friend)
   All losses are restor'd, and sorrows end.

WILLIAM SHAKESPEARE

When We Two Parted

When we two parted
    In silence and tears,
Half broken-hearted
    To sever for years,
Pale grew thy cheek and cold,
    Colder thy kiss;
Truly that hour foretold
    Sorrow to this.

The dew of the morning
    Sunk chill on my brow –
It felt like the warning
    Of what I feel now.
Thy vows are all broken,
    And light is thy fame:
I hear thy name spoken,
    And share in its shame.

They name thee before me,
    A knell to mine ear;
A shudder comes o'er me –
    Why wert thou so dear?
They know not I knew thee,
    Who knew thee too well: –
Long, long shall I rue thee,
    Too deeply to tell.

In secret we met –
　In silence I grieve,
That thy heart could forget,
　Thy spirit deceive.
If I should meet thee
　After long years,
How should I greet thee? –
　With silence and tears.

LORD BYRON

Wild Nights! Wild Nights!

Wild nights! Wild nights!
Were I with thee,
Wild nights should be
Our luxury!

Futile the winds
To a heart in port, –
Done with the compass,
Done with the chart.

Rowing in Eden!
Ah! the sea!
Might I but moor
To-night in thee!

EMILY DICKINSON

Acknowledgements

❧

The publishers gratefully acknowledge permission to reprint copyright material in this book as follows:

FLEUR ADCOCK: 'Against Coupling' reprinted with the permission of Bloodaxe Books on behalf of the author

ANNA AKHMATOVA: 'We Don't Know How to Say Goodbye' from *Selected Poems* translated by Richard McKane (Bloodaxe Books, 2006). Reprinted with permission of Bloodaxe Books on behalf of the author

SIMON ARMITAGE: 'Let me put it this way' and 'To His Lost Lover' from *Book of Matches* (Faber & Faber, 1993) © Simon Armitage, reprinted by permission of Faber & Faber Ltd

EMILY BERRY: 'Letter to Husband' © Emily Berry, from *Dear Boy* (Faber & Faber, 2013) reprinted by permission of the publisher

JOHN BETJEMAN: 'In a Bath Teashop' and 'A Subaltern's Love Song' from *Collected Poems* reprinted by permission of John Murray

CHARLES CAUSLEY: 'My Young Man's a Cornishman' from *Collected Poems* (Macmillan) reprinted by permission of the Estate of Charles Causley

WENDY COPE: 'Rondeau Redoublé' from *Making Cocoa for Kingsley Amis* (Faber & Faber, 1986) and 'Two Cures for Love' from *Two Cures for Love* (Faber & Faber, 2009) reprinted by permission of the publisher

E. E. CUMMINGS: 'anyone lived in a pretty how town', 'i carry your heart with me(i carry it in)' and 'somewhere I have never travelled,gladly beyond' © The Estate and reprinted by permission of W. W. Norton

MAURA DOOLEY: 'Freight' reprinted with permission of Bloodaxe Books on behalf of the author

[187]

CAROL ANN DUFFY: 'Valentine' and 'Warming Her Pearls' ©
Carol Ann Duffy (1993 and 1987), by permission of the poet
and Rogers, Coleridge & White

DOUGLAS DUNN: 'Modern Love' and 'Re-reading Katherine
Mansfield's *Bliss and Other Stories*' by permission of the poet
and United Agents

T. S. ELIOT: 'La Figlia Che Piange' and 'The Love Song of J.
Alfred Prufrock' reprinted by permission of Faber & Faber Ltd

GAVIN EWART: 'The Lover Writes a One-Word Poem' © Estate
of Gavin Ewart by kind permission of Mrs Margot Ewart

U. A. FANTHORPE: 'Atlas' from *New and Selected Poems*
(Enitharmon, 2010) by kind permission of Dr R. V. Bailey

JAMES FENTON: 'Hinterhof' and 'In Paris with You' reprinted by
permission of Faber & Faber Ltd

W. S. GRAHAM: 'I Leave This at Your Ear' from *Malcolm
Mooney's Land* (1970) and 'To My Wife at Midnight' from
Collected Poems (1979) reprinted in *New Collected Poems*
(Faber & Faber, 2004) © The Estate of W. S. Graham,
reprinted by permission of Faber & Faber Ltd

ROBERT GRAVES: 'Counting the Beats', 'Love Without Hope' and
'A Slice of Wedding Cake' from *Robert Graves Complete
Poems in One Volume* (Carcanet Press Ltd) by kind permission
of Carcanet Press

LAVINIA GREENLAW: 'Skin Full' and 'Tryst' © Lavinia Greenlaw
from *A World Where News Travelled Slowly* (Faber & Faber,
1997) reprinted by permission of the publisher

THOM GUNN: 'Tamer and Hawk' reprinted by permission of
Faber & Faber Ltd

IAN HAMILTON: 'Remember This' from *Collected Poems* edited
by Alan Jenkins (Faber & Faber, 2009) reprinted by permission
of the publisher

SEAMUS HEANEY: 'The Otter' and 'The Skunk' © The Estate of
Seamus Heaney, from *Field Work* (Faber & Faber, 1979)
reprinted by permission of the publisher

ADRIAN HENRI: 'Adrian Henri's Talking After Christmas Blues'
© Adrian Henri. Reproduced by permission of the Estate of
Adrian Henri c/o Rodgers, Coleridge & White

Group (USA) Inc., Gerald Duckworth & Co Ltd., Pollinger Limited and The National Association of the Advancement of Coloured People

KATHLEEN RAINE: 'The Ring' from 'The Marriage of Psyche' in *The Collected Poems* by permission of the Estate of Kathleen Raine

JO SHAPCOTT: 'Muse' © Jo Shapcott from *Her Book* (Faber & Faber, 1999) reprinted by permission of the publisher

MURIEL STUART: 'In the Orchard' © The Estate of Muriel Stuart by kind permission of the Estate

A. S. J. TESSIMOND: 'Black Monday Lovesong', 'First Meeting' and 'Not Love Perhaps' from *Collected Poems* (Bloodaxe Books, 2010). Reprinted with permission of Bloodaxe Books

HUGO WILLIAMS: 'Bar Italia' and 'Blindfold Games' © Hugo Williams from *Billy's Rain* (Faber & Faber, 1999) reprinted by permission of the publisher

MARY WILSON: 'The Train' from *New Poems* (Hutchinson, 1979)